SARTRE'S PHILOSOPHY OF SOCIAL EXISTENCE

MODERN REVIVALS IN PHILOSOPHY
Series Editor: Dr David Lamb

David Archard
Marxism and Existentialism: The Political Philosophy of Sartre and Merleau-Ponty
(0 7512 0051 4)

L Jonathan Cohen
The Probable and the Provable
(0 7512 0011 5)

David E Cooper
Authenticity and Learning: Nietzsche's Educational Philosophy
(0 7512 0012 3)

Jorge A Larrain
Marxism and Ideology
(0 7512 0013 1)

Jorge A Larrain
A Reconstruction of Historical Materialism
(0 7512 0048 4)

Jorge A Larrain
The Concept of Ideology
(0 7512 0049 2)

D G C Macnabb
David Hume: His Theory of Knowledge and Morality
(0 7512 0014 X)

Richard J Norman
Hegel's Phenomenology: A Philosophical Introduction
(0 7512 0015 8)

Anthony O'Hear
Experience, Explanation and Faith
(0 7512 0052 2)

John O'Neill
Sociology as a Skin Trade: Essays towards a reflexive sociology
(0 7512 0016 6)

John O'Neill (ed)
Modes of Individualism and Collectivism
(0 7512 0050 6)

Stephen Priest (ed)
Hegel's Critique of Kant
(0 7512 0064 6)

R A Sharpe
Contemporary Aesthetics
(0 7512 0017 4)

George J Stack
Kierkegaard's Existential Ethics
(0 7512 0018 2)

George J Stack
Sartre's Philosophy of Social Existence
(0 7512 0058 1)

W H Walsh
Metaphysics
(0 7512 0019 0)

W H Walsh
Reason and Experience
(0 7512 0020 4)

Deirdre Wilson
Presuppositions and Non-Truth-Conditional Semantics
(0 7512 0021 2)

SARTRE'S PHILOSOPHY OF SOCIAL EXISTENCE

George J Stack
Professor of Philosophy
State University of New York
Brockport

Gregg Revivals

© Warren H. Green, Inc 1977
© George J Stack 1992

All rights reserved

First published in Great Britain in 1977 by
Warren H Green, Inc

Reprinted in 1992 by
Gregg Revivals
Gower House
Croft Road
Aldershot
Hampshire GU11 3HR
England

Gregg Revivals
Distributed in the United States by
Ashgate Publishing Company
Old Post Road
Brookfield
Vermont 05036
USA

A CIP catalogue record for this book is available
from the British Library

A CIP catalogue record for this book is available
from the US Library of Congress

ISBN 0 7512 0058 1

Printed in Great Britain by Billing & Sons Ltd, Worcester.

PREFACE

The emergence of Jean-Paul Sartre as a social philosopher has been seen by some as a curious enigma, an abandonment of his passionate defense of individual freedom in *Being and Nothingness* and related works. Some interpreters of Sartre's later thought have taken up the theme of a "radical conversion" to a form of revisionist Marxism. Although I believe there is some substance to such readings of Sartre's *Critique de la raison dialectique*, there is the additional question of the possible continuity in the thought of Sartre from his phenomenological ontology to his dialectical social phenomenology. It is with this issue that I will primarily be concerned in an attempt to understand the origin and derivation of Sartre's phenomenology of social relations.

An attempt will be made to show that the internal development of Sartre's phenomenological descriptions of the world for consciousness, of concrete relations with others, and of concrete human freedom "in situation" led him in the direction of a consideration of human existence in social reality. In what may be called the dialectical development of Sartre's philosophical reflections, there is a consistent movement from a concern with the abstract freedom of man as consciousness to a growing concern with the relationship between the concrete freedom of the individual and the field of social determinations.

The projection of man as a free individual who "makes himself" through the pursuit of projects realized in action into a complex network of reciprocal, dialectical social relations seems to involve a gradual erosion of Sartre's conception of man's original freedom. To my mind, there is discernible in the phenomenology of social existence in the *Critique* a tendency to introduce not only deterministic factors impinging upon indidividual freedom, but a kind of necessity. It is as if Sartre has come to believe that individuals must renounce at least some degree of freedom in order to act in concert with others for the sake of the liberation of all men from repression, injustice and the inertia of social forces. To be sure, the problem Sartre deals with in the *Critique* is not as one-dimensional as this. For, there is a dialectical tension between the individual and society as a whole, as well as between the individual and social groups or classes. Sartre's intention, in his description of the complex dialectical relationships in social processes, is to illustrate, in Hegelian fashion, the way in which human freedom is preserved and negated in the socio-historical milieu. It is not so much that he desires to indicate the reconciliation between freedom and determinism in social action, but, rather, to reveal — by virtue of phenomenological description or the description of social phenomena "from within" as they are encountered in lived-experience — the complex interaction between individual freedom and materio-social determinations, interiority and exteriority, subjectivity and objectivity. In these intentions, it is contended, Sartre is fundamentally faithful to his earlier phenomenology of concrete freedom in situation. In effect, it will be suggested that the perspective of the *Critique* is, in many respects, implicit in the phenomenological ontology of human reality in relation to others and in concrete situations.

Aside from this general account of the continuity of Sartre's thought, I will be concerned with an attempt to show the influence of Georges Gurvitch's "existential sociology" on Sartre's conception of the social dialectic. The key to the description of the network of dialectical relations in the *Critique* is, I believe, found in Gurvitch's general notion of a "dialectical hyperempiricism." Although I am aware that Gurvitch's sociology and the social philosophy of Sartre are in the stream of post-Marxian thought in France, I believe that it is possible to attain an understanding of the social dialectic independent of a consideration of the details of Marx's general conception of dialectical processes in society. Indeed, the question of the precise relationship between Sartre's understanding of, and use of, a dialectical method of interpreting social phenomena or social processes and that of Marx is one that still remains despite the number of recent studies of Sartre's Marxism. At any rate, the discussion of the background of the formulation of a social dialectic serves as a prelude to a critical analysis of Sartre's sociological descriptions and a consideration of the implications of these descriptions for a conception of the free *praxis* of individuals in a social context.

This approach to a critical understanding of the development of Sartre's conception of man as a social being will begin with a consideration of the abstract freedom of consciousness as pure negativity and the world for consciousness. It will be suggested that the movement of Sartre's thought from an analysis of the immediate structure of consciousness (or the "for itself") to a description of concrete relations with others and concrete freedom in situation led him to provide an incomplete phenomenology of existence in community with others. It was an amplification of the description of man's concrete freedom that brought Sartre to the point of considering the nature of our being-with-others.

The second stage of this analysis will focus attention on the phenomenology of the encounter with others. It will be suggested that the reciprocal dialectical relationships between individuals described in the *Critique* has its roots in Sartre's previous understanding of our experience of others and our existence for others. It will be argued that there is an implicit dialectical relation between man and man in *Being and Nothingness* which finds its fulfillment in the more detailed analyses of this relation in the *Critique de la raison dialectique*. An attempt will be made to discern the threads of continuity in Sartre's understanding of concrete relations with others that extend from his earlier phenomenological ontology to his constructive description of man's relationship to others in a social milieu. It will be shown, I believe, that Sartre's conception of our concrete relationships to others has not radically changed since *Being and Nothingness*. Insofar as there is a modification of emphasis in the treatment of human encounters in a social world, it is a subtle shift from an abstract description of the relation between self and others to a more concrete description of such a relation in the actuality of social existence. This shift of emphasis is consonant with the parallel shift of perspective from a focus upon an abstract isolated consciousness to a concern with an individual's concrete experience in situations of facticity. To the factual or material situation illuminated by consciousness has been added — on the foundation of being-for-others — a dimension of existence in a social situation in which one encounters what Sartre describes as the "coefficient of adversity in men." The movement of Sartre's philosophical reflections proceeds from a description of the experience of others in which the ground of society is imperceptible to a clarification of concrete human relationships within the total social context which is given a prominent place in the humanized world in which man exercises his individual *praxis*. The communal world which was only touched upon in the concluding portions of *Being and Nothingness* becomes, in Sartre's social thought, the starting-point in the *Critique* for an understanding of the human condition in socio-historical reality.

The third stage in the development of my interpretation of Sartre's social phenomenology deals primarily with an elucidation of the conception of a social dialectic or dialectical experience in relation to the notion of a "dialectical hyperempiricism" as formulated by Georges Gurvitch. It will be shown that the dialectical sociology of Gurvitch is the primary key to an understanding of the form that Sartre's dialectic of social relations takes. Aside from a general consideration of Gurvitch's conception of "total social phenomena," an examination of Sartre's notion of the nature of dialectical experience is offered in order to grasp what I believe is the central constructive theme of the *Critique*. It will be contended that the description of social reality in terms of a complex network of reciprocal dialectical relationships is a plausible interpretation of social processes, of the relations between individuals, between groups and the dialectical relations between individuals within groups and the group itself.

Ideally, the discussion of what Sartre calls "the living logic of action" should be seen as superimposed upon the bases carried forward from the analyses of the world for consciousness, concrete relations with others, and the freedom of man in situation. The transition to the elucidation of a social dialectic involves an attempt to understand the essence of Sartre's approach to social phenomena in his own terms. In spite of his commitment to a form of Marxian historical materialism, I believe it is possible to comprehend Sartre's variation on the theme of dialectical sociology apart from the rather general notion of historical materialism. The dialectic of *praxis* is central to the notion of dialectical experience and is intelligible as a heuristic presupposition in a sociological analysis of any type of social process. The interaction of the individual with the *determinations partielles* encountered in a practical field is a central theme in Sartre's endeavor to determine the conditions for the possibility of a social philosophy and it is one which clearly indicates his sympathy with the fully developed sociology of Gurvitch. It is for this reason, of course, that the central principles and concepts of Gurvitch's existential sociology are examined by way of transition to a critical discussion of Sartre's theory of group dynamics. In this regard, the overall development of my interpretation of the later Sartre proceeds from a setting of the stage for the background which his own phenomenological ontology provides to the sociological bases of his interesting conception of an immanent social dialectic. Once the lines of continuity from *Being and Nothingness* to the *Critique* have been discerned as far as this is possible, it is assumed that they are incorporated, in a dialectical fashion, in the development of a theory of dialectical experience and are presumably preserved in the analysis of social serialities, groups-in-fusion and organized groups.

The final phase of this analysis will be primarily concerned with what I believe to be the internal tendency of Sartre's social phenomenology. That is, the apparently counter-intentional implication that the individual action which is presumably "the mover of everything" is absorbed and curtailed in group participation. Presumably, Sartre (like Gurvitch) intended to develop a description of social processes which would find a significant place for the innovative, spontaneous freedom of the individual. What I believe is actually discoverable in the elaborate and detailed descriptions of group-formation in the *Critique* is a subtle and gradual undermining of the power or importance of individual action. A concomitant element in the analysis of the structure of groups and the function of the individual member of a group is a shift of perspective from a description of the dialectical stages in the development of dynamic groups to a tendency to *prescribe* forms of social organization. The *dialectique* of individual *praxis* is quite free of prescriptive (if not of hypothetical and constructive) characteristics and is a careful tracing of the reciprocal relations amongst individuals in society, as well as being a lucid analysis of the paradoxical character of man's interactions with a social milieu and the material world.

On the other hand, the treatment of the coercive power of groups, as well as the socially instituted threat of violence, seems to lead Sartre away from some of the emphases of *Being and Nothingness* towards a social world in which the individual submerges his existential freedom in the purposive action of the group. Although there are occasional instances in which Sartre seems to mitigate such an interpretation of his concept of organized groups, there is an uneasy sense that we are gradually introduced to a prescription for group solidification and concerted action which seems to leave little room for individual expression of freedom within highly structured, purposive groups. It would seem as if Sartre has come to realize that the atomistic individual cannot, through his own power, bring about significant social change, insure social justice or negate the negation of scarcity. This is to say that it seems as though there is a tension in Sartre's social phenomenology between the espousal of the value and efficacy of individual *praxis* and the recognition of the powerful momentum and clear effectiveness of group *praxis*. Again, I do not claim that it is Sartre's intention to abandon the centrality of the agency of the free individual; rather, this process of mitigating the efficacy of individual freedom in a social milieu is implied in his conception of group functions and group dynamics. It is as if his attempt to project the existential freedom of man into the network of dialectical forces in society placed a preservation of human freedom in society in jeopardy independent of his original intention in the *Critique*.

Finally, within the context of a treatment of the phenomenology of group-formation, it is argued that there are lacunae in Sartre's sociology which seem to indicate the absence of an adequate consideration of the role of leadership in group organization and of the irrational factors which affect social action. In this regard, I am concerned with specifying what I consider to be defects in Sartre's sociological descriptions of the nature of, and action of, social groups. This is not to say that Sartre's social phenomenology is, in general, inaccurate or without any lasting value. On the contrary, it seems to me that Sartre has made an important contribution to the conflict paradigm of sociological interpretation and to the development of a philosophical sociology. That he has not yet completed the second volume of the *Critique* (that was to deal with a structural anthropology and the problem of history) does not undermine the value of the insights and theoretical explorations of the *Critique*.

Although it is undeniable that Sartre's social thought is informed by a desire to revitalize Marxism or to reconcile his own existential philosophy with a revised Marxism, I believe that it must not be forgotten that he has said that a "philosophy of freedom" will eventually take the place of Marxism. Perhaps the elements of such a philosophy are already implicitly present in a social phenomenology which preserves "the unsurpassable singularity of the human adventure." The tension between this desire and the desire to describe man as being-in-a-group subject to a multiplicity of inertial social and material forces is the central focus of attention in the *Critique*. Social structures and technological instruments are seen by Sartre as placing a screen between man and man, as barriers preventing a mutual understanding amongst men. His intention in the *Critique* seems to be to understand the material and social forces which prohibit the liberation of men, to understand the dialectical processes of social existence in order that some men may surpass them. There is no utopian optimism in Sartre's social philosophy, but, rather, there is an attempt to understand the various dimensions of human existence in the humanized world of social existence. Sartre's understanding of the individual within a social milieu tends to reveal a general tendency towards a crystallization of a social order which seems to undermine man's freedom and which stimulates attempts to revolt against this crystallized order. In turn, successful transformations of society tend towards a rigid institutionalization which negates the very freedom that was to be preserved. This general rhythm of social existence is also revealed in the local developments of social groups. The paradoxical tension between individual freedom and social crystallization is, then, the central phenomenon for Sartre's understanding of man in society. The *Critique* is a work which reveals a dialectic of oppositions which is not mediated by any facile synthesis.

In Raymond Aron's *Marxism and the Existentialists*, it is said that the analyses of the *Critique* may be of interest to philosophers, but that they offer nothing of significance to sociologists. To my mind, Sartre's *Critique* is a valuable study of the condition of man as a social being which has contributions to make to philosophers concerned with man as a sociohistorical individual and also provides a philosophically informed sociology which is an amplification of previously developed existential sociologies. Beneath the abstract terminology of the *Critique* there is a moral passion which shows that, for Sartre himself, man is not a useless passion. That Sartre has attempted to elucidate the general form of man's socially determined existence does not mean that he has abandoned his existential humanism or has adopted a purely sociological orientation towards man and his world. Rather, he has endeavored to give a dialectical account of the human world in which the relations amongst men are the most significant factors in the singular adventure of human life which, in Sartre's view, lies at the heart of history.

What Sartre calls the "dialectic of the subjective and the objective" is clearly an extension of a central theme in *Being and Nothingness* which is given a place in the *Critique* in terms of the concept of *praxis*. For, *praxis* is described as a passage or movement from objective to objective through the medium of "internalization." The subjective origin of intentional *praxis* is itself a dynamic unity of the subjective and the objective. The "lived experience" of individuals in society expresses itself in a process of objectification. As in *Being and Nothingness* (in the analysis of concrete human freedom), the *nisus* of the individual is from subjectivity to an objectification of this internal subjective project which creates and elucidates meanings in the concrete world. The tendency to surpass the limitations of objectivity is a central characteristic of man as such and of man as a social agent in particular. These general themes lie at the heart of Sartre's philosophical reflections and appear, as I attempt to indicate, in a slightly different perspective in the *Critique* than in *Being and Nothingness*. There is to be found in the *Critique de la raison dialectique* both a continuity with the earlier existential phenomenology and a difference which emerges in the situating of man in a practical social field. The intentionality of consciousness or the *pour-soi* is, for example, presupposed in Sartre's account of the dialectic of a selfconscious *praxis* in society. Although I have not attempted to illustrate all of the lines of continuity from Sartre's early work to the *Critique*, I have tried to focus on those that I believe are central to his thought. If, on the other hand, I have not analyzed all of the differences between Sartre as phenomenological ontologist and Sartre as social philosopher, I have tried to focus upon the sociological themes which account for many of these differences.

CONTENTS

Preface v
I. THE WORLD FOR CONSCIOUSNESS 3
   Consciousness as Nothingness 4
   Negativities 11
   Projects and Concrete Action 16
II. FREEDOM AND EXISTENCE FOR OTHERS 29
   Existence for Others 30
   Social Dimensions of the Other 38
III. THE SOCIAL DIALECTIC 51
   Dialectical Hyperempiricism 54
   Social Determinism and Freedom 57
   Dialectical Reason 77
   Social Phenomena 85
IV. A PHENOMENOLOGY OF SOCIAL RELATIONS 100
   Critical Dialectic versus Dogmatic Dialectic 101
   Scarcity, Action, and Group Formation 108
   The Coercive Power of the Group 121
   Necessity and the Neglect of the Irrational 124
Selected Bibliography 140
Index 145

Sartre's Philosophy
of Social Existence

I. THE WORLD FOR CONSCIOUSNESS

Le monde est humain.
L'Être et le néant.

Although almost two decades separate Sartre's general ontology in *Being and Nothingness* and his *Critique de la raison dialectique*, there is a fundamental sense in which the former phenomenological analysis of "human reality" provides the background against which the latter dialectical and descriptive analysis of social relations can be understood. On the surface, it may appear that Sartre's implicit commitment to a revisionist Marxism precludes any reference to his earlier impassioned defense of the subjective existence of the individual. This surface impression is misleading insofar as Sartre still retains his earlier philosophical vocabulary, his personal pessimistic vision of human existence, his sensitivity to the immense complexity of the lived-experience of man. One of my intentions here will be to show, in some detail, how the perspective of his later phenomenology of individual action and group-formation is, in fact, implicit in many of his previous descriptions of consciousness, the concrete self, the relation between the self and the other, and the relationship between man's attempt to realize his projects in the milieu of the contingent, but resistant, world of "being-in-itself." Despite the different philosophical tone of the *Critique,* its sociological language, its Marxist orientation, it still retains a continuity with Sartre's basic philosophical perspective in *Being and Nothingness.*

The question upon which attention will be focused is not whether Sartre's ostensible "conversion" to a form of Marxism does not undermine his existential phenomenology, but whether there is a discernible continuity in Sartre's philosophical thought which is the essential ingredient of his "transcendental" analysis of the conditions for the possibility of social existence. That there is such a fundamental continuity in Sartre's thought is, in itself, something worthy of consideration and would dispel the impression that there is a bifurcation between Sartre as existentialist *par excellence* and Sartre as dialectical social philosopher. It will be argued, at any rate, that there is implicit in Sartre's phenomenological ontology the "seeds" of his phenomonology of social processes and of his description of the role of human *praxis*. It is possible to interpret Sartre's social philosophy without engaging in ideological disputes or without recourse to psychological speculations about his "radical conversion" to Marxism or the history of his political sentiments. In this sense, I intend to focus upon philosophical rather than biographical or political concerns. The initial problem, then, is to try to discover — in the tangled web of Sartre's fundamental ontology of human reality — the theoretical basis for his dialectical sociology.

Consciousness as Nothingness

The most formidable obstacle confronting anyone who would seek a basic continuity in Sartre's thought is his radical conception of consciousness or the *pour-soi* in *Being and Nothingness*. This is especially the case insofar as the description of social relations, social phenomena, and social processes in the *Critique* seems to have jettisoned the notion that consciousness or the "for-itself" is the primordial origin of human freedom. What is required, then, is to show that Sartre's radical conception of consciousness is, to some extent, already put out of action, as it were, in *Being and Nothingness* itself. That is, that Sartre himself, once he has argued that "nothingness" emerges in the world by virtue of the negative structure of consciousness, tends to move from a conception of a primordial consciousness which is pure freedom to the concrete description of consciousness as manifested in the projects and actions of "human reality" or the individual self. Clearly, the implicit dualism in *Being and Nothingness* between consciousness and the impenetrable "being-in-itself" which surrounds man is no longer a dominant theme in his later phenomenology of social existence. It is as if he himself had seen that the ideal, abstract freedom of a consciousness exempt from all determination by virtue of its very structure was a merely theoretical freedom, a purely negative freedom which implied nothing about the possibility of man's free action or *praxis* in an actual world. That is, he had come to emphasize that the only meaningful freedom for man is a concrete freedom which can endeavor to act upon the world, to change the world in accordance with a subjective teleology. But this is not an entirely new approach to human freedom for Sartre since the phenomenological ontology he developed seems to have led ineluctably to such a conception of concrete freedom.

In his general argument in defense of the conception of the "for-itself" as no-thing, Sartre seems to proceed from the significant functions or activities of consciousness as such to its fundamental nature. In this regard, the description of the distinction between consciousness and being-in-itself in *Being and Nothingness* was already implicit in his conception of consciousness in *L'Imagination* "as spontaneous activity" directed outward towards the surrounding world.[1] It is clearly the primacy of imagination in Sartre's thought which determined his general analysis of the negative characteristic of consciousness. For, imagination is described as "an act which . . . aims at an absent or inexistent object by means of a physical or psychical continuant which is not given in itself, but [which is given] in the guise of an 'analogical representative' of the object aimed at."[2] Imagination, as one of the dominant or revealing aspects of consciousness, is a projective awareness of "what is not," of *le néant*. The nihilating or negating function of consciousness is primarily based upon the model of the activity of imagination. Throughout Sartre's phenomenology, the relationship between consciousness and facticity, consciousness and the world, is established by means of negating acts of consciousness. The general form of this theory of being and the dominant modes of being emerged out of his previous analyses of imagination in *L'Imagination* and *L'Imaginaire*. For, *Being and Nothingness* (at least initially) retains the distinction between consciousness and its objects, between that which exists "for itself" and is nothing without its correlate or that which exists "in itself." In order to avoid his earlier inclination to philosophical idealism, Sartre insists upon the independent existence of "being-in-itself" even though he continues to retain the fundamental phenomenological notion of Husserl that the meaning *(Sinn)* of being-in-itself is determined or constituted by the "for itself" or consciousness.

Despite his repeated insistence upon the non-being of consciousness, Sartre never abandons Husserl's notion that all consciousness is consciousness of something or that it posits a "transcendent object."[3] Paradoxically, a consciousness which is presumably "nothing" is described as having a distinctive "dimension of being" and as capable of a variety of acts, including that of "nihilation." In this sense, Sartre, *malgré lui*, retains his own version of intentional consciousness as capable of various "performances" or "accomplishments" *(Leistungen)* in the sense in which Husserl conceived of the function of consciousness. But, rather than assuming consciousness as a primal posit which is the basis of constitutive knowledge or intelligible experience, Sartre takes the drastic step of describing the "for itself" as a nothingness which is, nevertheless, capable of spontaneity. To my mind, there are two fundamental reasons why Sar-

---

1. Jean-Paul Sartre, *L'Imagination*, Paris, 1936, pp. 1-3
2. Jean-Paul Sartre, *L'Imaginare*, Paris, 1940, p. 75
3. Jean-Paul Sartre, *L'Être et le néant*, Paris, 1943, p. 17

tre was led to formulate this extreme conception of the nature of consciousness. The primary reason, as I have already suggested, is that he reasons from the function of imagination to the "being" which is capable of acts of imagination. For, he had argued that in imagination we posit an image which is a construct of consciousness; this activity involves the negation of the real. The denial that an imagined object (or, for that matter, a sequence of events) belongs to the real is tantamount to negating the real by positing this object. Through such intentional acts of consciousness (specifically, acts of imagination), man is able to bring what "is not" into the world. For Sartre, then, imagination is the paradigmatic form of 'nihilation.' But what is defective in this interpretation of the being of consciousness in terms of its capacity to create and apprehend negativity is that it ignores the dependence of imagination on previous sensation or perceptual experience. For, without a recollection of sensations or perceptions already experienced, imagination would lack a content and would, strictly speaking, be impossible. Thus, it is more plausible to assume that consciousness is capable of intending sensory experiences prior to its later capacity to construct the "non-existent." To be sure, the receptivity of consciousness to external impressions or stimuli does suggest a passivity which one might describe in negative terms. But in the spontaneous activity of consciousness—in, for example, what Husserl called "intentional shifts" —the agency of an actual entity or process is undeniable. The translucency of consciousness in spontaneous activity does present a real difficulty for an ontology of consciousness, but it does not entail the view that consciousness is "nothingness." Consciousness, as a generalized awareness, does, as Sartre says, seem to "surge" forward towards a multiplicity of phenomena, to "become," as Aristotle suggested, its intended objects. Its being does not appear to be "like" the phenomena which it attends to or knows. In this sense, consciousness is not a phenomenon, not an object, and not a thing. And yet its relational being seems to be intermediate between non-being and the beings which are disclosed to it. The "lack" *(manque)* which Sartre attributes to consciousness has an element of plausibility insofar as pure consciousness, without a determinate content, appears to be precisely a negativity. The problem seems to be that Sartre attempts, in *Being and Nothingness,* to treat original consciousness in a kind of abstract isolation and, for this reason, is led to describe its being in purely negative terms.

Sartre's theoretical analysis of the structure of consciousness assumes the form it does because of his persistent tendency to understand consciousness in light of the "nihilating" activity of imagination and because of his treatment of the "for itself" in a kind of artificial, purely hypothetical isolation. As has recently been said:

> One might be tempted . . . to try to reach consciousness in itself, isolated from everything, allowing ourselves to perform an unjustifiable abstraction. We already know that consciousness is always consciousness of something and that it can therefore not be separated from being [in itself].[4]

In Sartre's phenomenology, the negative mode of being of consciousness is gradually eroded as his analysis proceeds in the direction of facticity and concreteness; that is, its positive constitutive function comes more and more to the fore despite the fact that he continues to refer back to consciousness as "nothingness." The reason for this, as I shall attempt to show, is that the being of consciousness is only truly revealed in and through bodily existence and the activity of the self. In the immanent relationship between consciousness and an active individual, the true nature of consciousness is manifested. In the lived-experience of an individual consciousness is not a pure negation, but is a dynamic activity, a living consciousness. To be sure, the intentionality of consciousness is never abandoned, and is a function of consciousness which will continue to play a significant role in terms of the positing of projects or ends for individual *praxis* in the social dimension of human life.

There is a second reason why Sartre conceives of the "for itself" in the way he does; it is, however, one which is more speculative than that already suggested. One reason why Sartre seems to insist upon the "nothingness" of consciousness is his persistent interest in preserving human freedom from the nets of determinism as he understands it. It is as if Sartre thought that a conception of consciousness as a positive entity would preclude the possibility of describing man as free. The for-itself is sometimes described as the origin of human freedom and, at other times, it is described as freedom itself. What Berdyaev has described as *meonic* freedom is tantamount to the notion of the nothingness of consciousness as the foundation of human freedom. Thus, for example, freedom, choice, nihilation and temporalization are, at one point in *Being and Nothingness*, related to the indeterminate nothingness of consciousness.[5] The pure unconditioned freedom of consciousness is assumed to be the only basis for human freedom. In this sense, it is Sartre's conception of determinism — which, in point of fact, is actually a form of necessitarianism — which conditions his radical description of consciousness. For, Sartre seems

---

4. René Lafarge, *Jean-Paul Sartre: His Philosophy*, trans. M. Smyth-Kok, Notre Dame, 1970, p. 37.
5. J. P. Sartre, *op. cit.*, p. 543.

to have believed that neither freedom nor possibility could find a place in a deterministic universe in which every event (even that of a choice) would be construed as having a cause. Only by conceiving of consciousness as free from all possible determinations could Sartre conceive of man as free. In this respect, his existentialist conception of freedom is more radical than that of Kierkegaard.[6] His treatment of human facticity reveals, as I shall try to indicate, that he is, in fact, quite aware of the conditioning factors which impinge upon human freedom. And, in the *Critique,* this sense of the empirical limitations of free action receives even more pronounced emphasis. The point is that Sartre conceived of determinism as a kind of universal doctrine of necessity which precluded freedom of choice or action and, for this reason, put forward a theory of human freedom based upon the non-being of consciousness. In the *Critique,* he is far more willing to admit that there are real determining factors which curtail man's freedom without negating it, to acknowledge that the empirical world and its effects upon the individual do not undermine man's actual *finite* freedom. In *Being and Nothingness,* on the other hand, it would seem that he could conceive of no other way of preserving human freedom than by assuming that "freedom is actually one with the being of the for-itself; human reality is free to the extent that it has to be its own nothingness."[7] But this freedom itself remains nothing but a kind of abstract freedom, a directionless "original freedom." And it is certainly not necessary to develop an ontology of "absolute freedom" in order to retain the view that man is responsible for his choices, decisions, or actions. Even in his early phenomenological ontology, Sartre is led to admit that the only meaningful freedom man can have is a freedom to bring about change in the *actual* world, to overcome the obstacles present in the impenetrable world of the "in itself." But, it is clear that such an exercise of freedom *in the world* necessarily entails the view that causal factors over which the individual has no control will be encountered. That there are such factors impinging upon the life of an individual does not mean, by any means, that there is no possiblity nor does it mean that freedom for choice, freedom of choice, and freedom of action are not possible. Since Sartre holds that man does not "posit" or create the world (as in idealism), and since he insists in his discussion of "Being and Doing" that freedom would lose its meaning if the exteriority of "things" was not real and independent of consciousness, he clearly did not have to

---

6. Cf. George J. Stack, "The Basis of Kierkegaard's Concept of Existential Possibility," *New Scholasticism,* Spring, 1972, pp. 139-172.
7. J. P. Sartre, *op. cit.,* p. 529: "Nous avons montré que la liberté ne faisait qu'un avec l'être du pour-soi: la réalité humaine est libre dans l'exacte mesure où elle a à être son propre néant."

resort to the extreme notion that man, as consciousness, is nothingness. But, what seems to have haunted his thinking in describing the fundamental modes of being was a concept of determinism which precluded freedom or possibility. This, I believe, was one determining factor in his formulation of a radical and questionable conception of human consciousness.

Just as Kant had argued that man, as a rational moral agent, is free from natural determinations, so, too, does Sartre conceive of the being of consciousness as exempt from a causal order. The initiation of projects is a free, spontaneous act of being-for-itself in its capacity to surpass, through negation of an actual state of affairs, the conditioning factors which affect the mode of being of things in themselves. Negation is not merely a property or quality of judgements, but is prereflective and prejudmental; it emerges in the world by virtue of the ontological structure of consciousness itself. For Sartre, every conscious, intentional act involves a nihilation of something and thereby the possible emerges as a basis for surpassing the actual. Whereas Kierkegaard (in *The Concept of Dread*) referred to the encounter with "the nothingness of possibility," Sartre traces the origin of the sense of possibility to the non-objective character of consciousness itself. The orientation of consciousness or the "for itself" towards the world (the structure of which, as we shall see, is dependent upon the activity of consciousness) is one of expectation or anticipation. Put in another way, the primary *nisus* of consciousness is towards the world and towards what is not yet. Nihilation is an activity of consciousness whereby the actual, independent being of beings-in-themselves is negated in order to be surpassed. Since consciousness is described as lacking self-sufficiency or self-identity, it may be said that it is, in Sartrean terms, "surging" forward towards what it is not. It is for this reason that Sartre insists that "all that there is of intention in my actual consciousness is directed toward the outside, toward the world . . . "[8] It is with this aspect of the intentionality of consciousness rather than with the immediate relationship of consciousness to itself, the complex distinctions between prereflective and reflective consciousness, that we will be primarily concerned insofar as the realization of freedom in concrete situations is the significant expression of human freedom in a social milieu. Already, in his phenomenological ontology, Sartre shifts his focus of attention from the internal modes of consciousness itself to the relationship between human consciousness and "being" and "doing." For, he ultimately concludes that the "for itself" or consciousness defines itself by action. It is in the transcendence of the self towards its own

---

8. J. P. Sartre, *op. cit.*, p. 19: ". . . tout ce qu'il y a d'intention dans ma conscience actuelle est dirigé vers le dehors, vers le monde . . . cette conscience spontaneé de ma preception est *constitutive* de ma conscience perceptive."

possibilities that the significant function of consciousness is shown. In Hegelian terms, one may say that Sartre's analysis of the "immediate structure of the for itself" is sublated (negated and preserved) in his subsequent analysis of man's concrete freedom.

Ab initio, Sartre had argued that consciousness is primarily *practical* consciousness, that human consciousness is invariably engaged. Thus, for example, in *The Transcendence of the Ego* he had held that "when I run after a street-car . . . there is no I. There is consciousness of the street-car-having-to-be overtaken."[9] However, even in such practical involvement or engagement, there is a consciousness of this conscious act as well as a simultaneous self-consciousness since prereflective consciousness is coeval with self-consciousness. But this is a non-positional, non-thetic consciousness of self as accompanying intentional acts of consciousness. The point Sartre wants to make is that the self is not a reflective object of knowledge in such various engagements of consciousness. In these terms, then, the significant engagement of consciousness is in relation to posited "objects" of consciousness which are not things as such but possibilities which one endeavors to realize. The "dimension of being" of consciousness as such implies the simultaneous positive existence of beings-in-themselves. Although Sartre claims (initially) that there is no relation between consciousness and beings-in-themselves, his subsequent analyses belie this claim and indicate a distinctive dialectical relationship between consciousness and positive, non-conscious being.

If such a relationship can be discerned, at least implicitly, in *Being and Nothingness,* then an ontological basis can be established for the relationship between individual action and the practical material field in which this action takes place. Although Sartre himself considers the possibility of a dialectical relationship between being and nothingness, he dismisses it. He does so because he claims that negation cannot "touch" the plenitude of being and because he assumes that "being is prior to nothingness and establishes the ground for it . . . it is from being that nothingness derives its efficacy."[10] No sooner has Sartre described the dependent origination of consciousness (as "nothingness") than he asserts the equiprimordial emergence of consciousness and being-in-itself. For, from the hypothetical, ideal perspective of Being as such — which Sartre ultimately refers to a metaphysical problematic — "the relation of the for-itself to the in-itself is a fundamental ontological relation." The "upsurge" of consciousness (which had previously been described in isolation from

---

9. J. P. Sartre, *The Transcendence of the Ego,* trans. F. Williams, New York, 1957, p. 49.
10. J. P. Sartre, *L'Être et le néant,* p. 52: ". . . l'être est antérieur au néant et le fonde . . . c'est de l'être que le néant tire concrètement son efficace."

things or beings-in-themselves) is something which also "happens" to the in-itself. For, the disclosure that "there is" the in-itself exists solely *in relation to* consciousness. That is, *il n'y a d' être que pour un Pour-soi* [*"there is* being only for a for-itself"].[11] In this sense, the *being* of things is only in relation to the existence of consciousness. In non-Sartrean terms we can say that the way in which things are understood, interpreted, valued or disvalued, used or ignored, etc., is decidedly relative to the intentional projects of the dynamic consciousness of man or "human reality." In Heideggerian language, we could say that the "as structure" of being-in-itself is referential to consciousness. For, the *meaning* of things (beings-in-themselves) can only be apprehended by consciousness. The in-itself is, to be sure, still wholly independent of consciousness; but it is clear that the world disclosed to consciousness is a complex system of meanings which is not given in the being of the in-itself. It is for this reason that he says that "the world is human" and that "man's relation to being is that he can modify it."[12] Before discussing the role of consciousness in concrete expressions of freedom in action, it is necessary to consider, briefly, Sartre's phenomenology of negations because of the reappearance of this description in the context of his attempt to discern the fundamental negativities affecting man's socio-historical existence.

Negativities

In his so-called regressive analysis *(régression analytique)* Sartre had attempted to begin with an analysis of the concrete in order to illuminate the theoretical question of the nature of consciousness and the fundamental origin of negativity. This method of analysis led him to a consideration of the apprehension of *soi-disant* "negative beings" or *négatités*. This aspect of Sartre's ontology is specifically related to our concern with a discernment of the relations among consciousness, "negative beings," and the intentional action of man as such. For, these relations lie at the heart of any understanding of the primary purpose of human *praxis*. The assumption that there are negativities encountered in human experience, in the world, is central to the later Sartrean notion that human action is an attempt to negate negations encountered in the world of actuality.

If, in Sartre's phenomenology, consciousness is disclosed to itself as no-thing, there are correlative negativities discovered in human experience, specifically in relation to "human expectation." The apprehension of such negations is originally based upon man's relationship to the world. Despite the attempt to show that there are real negativities en-

---
11. *Ibid.*, p. 268.
12. *Ibid.*, p. 62: "Ce qu'elle peut modifier, c'est son *rapport* avec cet être."

countered in intuitive experience and, hence, to indicate a prejudgmental basis for negative judgements, it would seem that Sartre only manages to show that such negativities can be discerned in relation to human consciousness.

Although there are presumably an "infinite" number of *négatités* which man can encounter, Sartre focuses upon distance, absence, interrogation, change, otherness, repulsion, regret, distraction, fragility, and destruction. Of these, he provides analyses of distance, absence, interrogation, destruction and fragility. Ostensibly, Sartre tries to describe the "intuitive discovery" of negative beings which presumably have an inner, negative structure in themselves. In fact, it is never convincingly shown that there are independent, "real" negative beings. What Sartre does indicate is that man is capable of the intentional recognition of negativities which are meaningful only in relation to consciousness.

While it may be granted that a consciousness of negativity (e.g., the absence of someone) does suggest the capacity of consciousness to apprehend negativities, it neither demonstrates that the origin of nothingness is the non-objective being of consciousness nor that there are real, independent and objective negative beings. In regard to the former problem it has recently been argued that:

> ... negative beings *(négatités)* are special cases, selected by an arbitrary guiding thread, and that, apart from such cases, consciousness is confronted with positive phenomena, such that the inference of a negative consciousness is unconvincing ... The analytic regress inferring an original negative, the subject, from a derivative negative, the phenomena, infers a ground for a given in one-sided interpretation from such given.[13]

That there is some equivocation in Sartre's analysis is clear from the way in which he gives different accounts of the 'nature' of negative beings in a number of illustrations. Thus, in some instances, he refers primarily to the negative index of some negativities and, in other instances, he emphasizes negativities which presumably contain a negative constituent. In his discussion of the objective of an artillery gunner, he remarks that this particular objective is revealed as fragile. This *fragilité* is the probability of the non-being for a given being under determined circumstances; that is, the objective has as its possibility a possibility of not being. However, this fragility is said to come into being through man. This is a curious illustration for Sartre to use insofar as what he says about the objective of the artillery gunner is true of *all* beings in themselves in the sense that each being-in-itself is purely contingent just as man himself is contingent. To be

---
13. Klaus Hartmann, *Sartre's Ontology*, Evanston, 1966, pp. 49-50.

sure, the possibility of the non-existence of any being does reveal a kind of negativity in such a being (as Hegel had previously argued in regard to the non-being in the being of man). But such contingency is, for the most part, *independent* of an individual consciousness. Thus, the fact that a particular falls is now being eroded to the point where it will be "negated" as a falls is a kind of negativity occurring in nature which is independent of human consciousness as such and, therefore, this "fragility" tells us nothing about the nature of consciousness itself. It is not "through man" that such instances of fragility come into being. Surely, in his own terms, Sartre must hold that the contingency of beings-in-themselves is itself independent of the nature or being of consciousness. In this case, we have discovered a negativity which is presumably independent of consciousness, but which reveals nothing about consciousness itself. In addition, of course, the very notion of the fragility of something (e.g., a waterfall) has meaning only in reference to something which is actual, but which is subject to the empirical possibility of being passively destroyed as what it was previously. Clearly, this case of a "negative being" does not serve Sartre's purpose too well.

Before returning to the residual question of whether Sartre has persuasively argued in defense of the notion of the independent existence of what he metaphorically calls "pools of non-being," we will consider what I believe is Sartre's strongest argument concerning the origin of negation. That is his claim that negation enters the world through interrogation or the posing of a question. In posing a question, he argues, we posit the possibility of a negative answer and, in a sense, we question a being about its being or its way of being. What we are presuming, it is said, is that an existent can be revealed as nothing. To be able to question we must be able to withdraw from the given or dissociate ourselves from a causal nexus. This detachment from being, this so-called "nihilating withdrawal," is a disengagement which is a "human process." By negating what is questioned man puts it "out of action" and places it in a "neutral state" while, at the same time, he negates himself *vis-à vis* the thing questioned by disengaging "himself from being in order to be able to bring out of himself the possibility of a non-being."[14] If we grant that raising a question about something (or some being) does bring about the emergence of "a certain negative element" in the world, does this mean that we must conclude that the activity of questioning is itself a "negative being" in the world?

---

14. J. P. Sartre, *L'Être et le néant*, pp. 59-60: "Cela signifie que, par un double mouvement de néantisation, il néantise le questionné par rapport à lui, en le plaçant dans un état neutre . . . et qu'il se néantise lui-même par rapport au questionné en s'arrachant à l'être pour pouvoir sortir de soi la possibilité d'un non-être."

Moreover, does this argument, as subtle as it is, commit us to the view that the consciousness which questions is itself negative? To be sure, interrogation is a mode of conduct for man and it does seem to reveal man's capacity to stand out of the "stream of experience" or disengage himself from prereflective involvement in a field of instrumental complexes. But, what is questioned continues to be actual except as neutralized through the nihilating activity of consciousness. Interrogation is a way in which man can comport himself towards beings, towards others, or towards himself, but it appears to be an activity of consciousness that presupposes some answer to a question (positive or negative) in reference to what *is* and not primarily in reference to what is not. In interrogation non-being is not disclosed as being as such. Like so-called negative facts, the negativity of interrogation presupposes an acquaintance with something that is (or, in the case of negative facts, an acquaintance with positive facts).

Questioning says something about a *function* of consciousness, but not necessarily something about the nature of consciousness. We may recognize the profundity of man's capacity to apprehend negation or express negation through questioning without admitting that, by virtue of this, "nothingness" arises in the world. If we admit that negation does exist in the world by virtue of the dual nihilations of consciousness, this negation still remains in relation to consciousness - it is a purely internal negation. Since the world *(le monde)* is said to come to be through the "upsurge of the for itself," and since the "objective structure of the world" is caused by the being of the for itself,[15] then Sartre cannot consistently hold that the dual nihilations of consciousness bring about the emergence of negation (as a 'reality') *in the world.* This is *a fortiori* the case if, as Sartre avers, the "world in which consciousness is engaged . . . comes into being through consciousness."[16] That is, unless one merely assumes *a priori* that consciousness is a nothingness which is, in some mysterious way, immanent in the world which exists in relation to consciousness.

Although the analysis of the meaning and form of negative beings could be considerably extended, the central point to be emphasized is the basic failure of Sartre to sustain the view that there are objective, independent real negativities "in the world." The correlation between consciousness and "nothingness" and "negative beings" is established solely on the basis of the referential nature of such *négatités*. This is made ex-

---

15. *Ibid.*, p. 525: " . . . c'est le surgissement du pour-soi fait qu'il y ait un monde . . . qui fait qu'il y ait une certaine structure objective du monde."
16. *Ibid.*, p. 521: ". . . le monde redoubtable où la conscience est engagée et qui vient à l'être par elle."

plicit in Sartre's account itself. For, he maintains that these "realities" . . .

> . . . all indicate immediately an essential relation of human reality to the world. They derive their origin from an act, an expectation, or a project of the human being; they all indicate an aspect of being as it appears to the human being who is engaged in the world.[17]

Not only is the consciousness of negativities inseparable from the "existence" of negativities, but our consciousness of the sharp outline of positive realities is possible by virtue of negation. The negativities dispersed in the world are especially significant in relation to two aspects of the concrete freedom of man: the transcending towards one's projects and one's own possibilities and the tendency to negate negations through action. It is the freedom of man (which is equated with "human reality") which "conditions the appearance of nothingness in the world." The existential possibilities of the self (or of consciousness projecting itself toward the self it is not yet) are focused upon as one's own possibilities insofar as rejected, alternative possibilities are negated—they are posited in order to be negated. The self-becoming of the individual, then, entails the negation of possibilities and the projection of ideal (non-existent) possibilities of being. The consciousness of such possibilities is necessarily an engagement in the world (comprised of negativities and a multiplicity of positive realities or beings); in concrete action "a structure of *exigency*" is disclosed in the world as comprised of a "complex of instrumentality."[18] The meaning of the phenomena disclosed in the world is subjectively determined. In addition, the value of these disclosed meanings is sustained by the freedom of the individual who chooses to value this or that. The meaning and value of the practical instrumental complex is sustained by the projects of individuals. This fundamental notion, in relation to the encounter with negativities in experience, will be retained by Sartre in his phenomenology of social existence or man's engagement in the practical field in which his action can have efficacy. The primary *négatité* which will dominate Sartre's conception of the pragmatic motivation of human action and the basis of conflict between nations, classes, groups and individuals is scarcity *(rareté)*. It is his belief that until this fundamental *négatité* is nihiliated — not by internal, but by external negation—struggle and conflict will be ineluctable.

---

17. *Ibid.*, p. 60.
18. *Ibid.*, p. 74.

Projects and Concrete Action

The transition from what might be called the abstract freedom of consciousness as such — which is free in its ostensible "negation" of the in-itself and in its negation of itself as well in the projection of possibilities — is brought about in Sartre's account of concrete freedom or, in other words, the relationship between the for-itself and human facticity. Sartre's analysis of consciousness reveals it to be the origin of negation, the basis for the apprehension and projection of possibilities (as inexistents), the foundation of the meanings of things disclosed in the world and the foundation of *le monde* or "the world" as such. The significance of everything is assumed to be referential to consciousness since beings-in-themselves have no intrinsic significance; rather, they are merely encountered as already *there*.

The abstract freedom of consciousness is, in Sartre's account, the primordial origin of human freedom even though the freedom of consciousness in its nihilating or negating capacity is a kind of empty freedom. It is a freedom which could be experienced by a man in solitary confinement as well as by the most liberated man of action. To be sure, Sartre seems aware of this even in his earliest analysis of the "immediate structure of the for itself." For, he remarks that the being of consciousness does not only have the "abstract characteristics" (e.g., nihilation or internal negation) he has attributed to it. Consciousness is continually engaged in the beings which surround it, is involved in its relation to beings as well as to possibilities. As Sartre expresses it:

> The concrete consciousness arises in situation, and it is a unique, individualized consciousness of this situation and (of) itself in situation. It is to this concrete consciousness that the self is present, and all the concrete characteristics of consciousness have their correlates in the totality of the self. The self is individual; it is the individual completion of the self which haunts the for-itself.[19]

Precisely what the for-itself lacks is the self; and human reality is concretely expressed by a transcendence towards what it lacks. This transcendence is manifested in the projects of individual consciousness, its movement, as it were, towards its possibilities. Consciousness, as apprehending negation, is the condition of the possibility of discovering or positing possibilities by which the self can become what it is not yet. In Sartre's terms, the self surpasses itself towards the world conceived of as the "totality of beings within the compass of the circuit of selfness."[20] We may say,

---

19. *Ibid.*, p. 134.
20. *Ibid.*, p. 148.

then, that consciousness discloses or posits possibilities, but it is concrete consciousness immanent in the self which is the basis for the *nisus* towards the realization of possibilities in the world. As Sartre puts it, "my possibility can exist as *my* possibility only if it is my consciousness which escapes itself [transcends itself] toward my possibility."[21]

In order to pass from the "absolute interiority" of consciousness, there must be a means by which this consciousness is immanently related to the facticity of the individual. The world which arises presumably by means of the "upsurge" of consciousness is coeval with my sense of being-in-the-world as a "psychic body" or, simply, as a psychophysical individual who "exists" his body. The for-itself or consciousness finds itself in situation as a presence to the world and is, in this sense, affected with facticity. The fact that the for-itself is not the ground of its being is its contingency. That is, consciousness "is sustained by a perpetual contingency for which it assumes the responsibility and which it assimilates without . . . being able to surpass it."[22] This "evanescent contingency" constitutes the facticity of the for-itself. This facticity is rooted in situation and in the world. That Sartre is here indicating a complex dialectical relationship between consciousness and being-in-itself is clear in his assertion that the contingency of consciousness is "derived from the in-itself."[23] In this preliminary account of the facticity of consciousness, Sartre has not yet related consciousness to concrete free action in situations in the world and, in this regard, his analysis is truncated. It is in his phenomenologies of the body and concrete freedom that the full meaning of the endeavor to realize projects or values is disclosed. The primacy of consciousness is still evident in these later analyses even though the interrelationship between consciousness and facticity clearly becomes more complex than Sartre had indicated in his attempt to provide a thorough phenomenology of consciousness. The possible "insurmountable dualism" to which Sartre's analyses of consciousness and being-in-itself seemed to lead is, in the final analysis, resolved by the relationship sustained between being-in-itself and consciousness by the for-itself. In his conclusion, Sartre makes an explicit statement which tends to undermine the radical bifurcation of consciousness and beings. For, he remarks that "the for-itself and the in-itself are reunited by a synthetic connection which is nothing other than the for-itself itself."[24] This is a conclu-

---

21. *Ibid.*, p. 128: "Ma possibilité ne peut exister comme ma possibilité que si c'est ma conscience qui s'eschappe à soi vers elle."
22. *Ibid.*, p. 125.
23. *Ibid.*, p. 127.
24. *Ibid.*, p. 711: ". . . le Pour-soi et l'En-soi sont réunis par une liaison synthetique qui n'est autre que le Pour-soi lui-même."

sion which is already implicit in Sartre's account of the complex relationship between consciousness and the transcendence towards projects or possibilities which the individual endeavors to realize through action in temporality, in the world, and in situations. The world, for Sartre, is consistently described as the world for us, for consciousness. But the facile synthetic connection between consciousness and the in-itself which Sartre proffers in his concluding remarks tends to bracket the ambiguity of the *interrelationship* between consciousness and beings which he discloses in his description of human action.

The for-itself is described as encountering a "horizon of possibilities" insofar as the self can never completely overcome its "lack" — that is, achieve a coincidence with itself — and insofar as the attainment of the possible will make the for-itself be as for-itself (i.e., as the repository of the possible). Due to the perpetual activity of negation, consciousness reveals to itself a multiplicity of possibilities. Self-realization, in Sartre's thought, is a perpetually fleeting goal which presumably is ended only by death. This is an ineluctable consequence of his definition of consciousness as being what it is not, being a "lack." However, the internal dialectic of consciousness is such that, as lacking something, it is impelled to action. This notion is analogous to Aristotle's dictum that there is no action without desire. Action has as its condition the apprehension of a "desideratum" — that is, "an objective lack" or a *négatité*. The *négatité* which is immanent in the being of consciousness is the "lack" or negation which it is possible, in a limited sense, to negate through concrete action. The objective being of things in the world (e.g., the factual state of the world or the factical beings in the world) can never provide, in itself, a motivation for action. No factual state of affairs can, *per se,* determine consciousness to see it as a lack or negativity. Whereas the negativity of "lack" is an essential aspect of the structure of consciousness, the apprehension of ostensible "objective negativities" requires a referential understanding of them *as* negativities for consciousness. Any human act is described by Sartre as an intentional "projection of the for-itself toward what is not,"[25] towards the possible.

In action, an individual negates competing possibilities and posits an end or *telos* which is to be attained. This subjective teleology expresses the three modi of temporality since the goal is projected into a non-existent future, but the cause or motive is derived from the past; the present is the "upsurge" of an act. The cause of an action is constituted by consciousness in the sense that it confers value on both the end pursued and the cause of the intentional action. Human freedom is discovered or learned in and

---

25. *Ibid.*, pp. 510-511: "... un acte est une projection du pour-soi vers ce qui n'est pas ..."

through action. Because of the primordial negativity of consciousness man is forced, as it were, to make himself, to create a self. But this movement towards the self one is not yet requires, in Sartre's view, a negation of being-in-itself. This involves a transcendence towards possibility and a transcendence of actuality insofar as the in-itself *is* actuality. Man defines his being through the pursuit of ends or goals and manifests his freedom by virtue of this. This transcendent projection of the will and passion of man towards his possibilities requires the negation of facticity itself. In rational action this is not accomplished by a magical withdrawal from the world (e.g., in fear, fainting, cataplexie, etc.), but by an active overcoming of obstacles encountered in the world. The rational existence of the self (which Sartre obviously considers the only meaningful mode of existence) requires a scientific appraisal of a factual situation, an attempt to resolve problems through the realization of a "determined series and instrumental complexes." That is, action should enable man to modify facticity in accordance with valued ends or goals.

In a concrete consciousness of intentional action, there is an intimate relationship of the self to what Heidegger (and Sartre after him) describes as "the world [as] a synthetic complex of instrumental realities as they point one to another in ever widening circles." To interpret the phenomena encountered in the world as an "organized totality" requires the surpassing of being-in-itself through negation. This negation or nihilation does not affect the in-itself as such, but it alters the way in which man apprehends the world. It is clear that Sartre obviously assumes that the world understood as a complex of instrumental actualities is the proper rational orientation of consciousness to intramundane entities. Yet, the meaning of the factual phenomena in the world presupposes that the concrete consciousness discovers such phenomena as instrumental things by means of a choice of itself as this individual projecting itself towards the world in this specific way. The particular meaning of phenomena is determined by the subjective projects of individuals. Man's original "ontological freedom" is ultimately brought to concrete fruition precisely in concrete action in relation to a field of facticities. Freedom in situation is not, for Sartre, "a pure, capricious, unlawful, gratuitous, and incomprehensible contingency."[26]

The concrete realization of human freedom is, in fact, manifested through bodily action insofar as Sartre explicitly states that consciousness is entirely body *and* entirely consciousness. Man's concrete being-in-the-world is expressly manifested in bodily existence. To be sure, an in-

---

26. *Ibid.*, p. 530.

dividual's body is an in-itself for others in its basic being-for-others, but as a lived-actuality it is "nothing other than the for-itself."[27] The body may be conceived of as inseparable from the situation in which consciousness is engaged. One could say, then, that the body is the medium by which concrete consciousness is engaged in the world and, as such, it is the vehicle of action. Although the directionality of an action and the continuation of an action is dependent upon the sustaining activity of consciousness, it is the "psychic body" which acts. The body as coextensive with the world is the foundation of man's being-in-the-world. Sartre relates these two aspects of human existence in the following way:

> ... my being-in-the-world, by the sole fact that it *realizes* a world, causes itself to be indicated to itself as a being-in-the-midst-of-the-world by the world which it realizes ... my being has no other way of entering into contact with the world except to be in the world ... that I have entered into the world ... or that there is a world, or that I have a body is one and the same thing.[28]

It is this consciousness-body which is the agent which can act in the world which appears as "objectively articulated," an "infinity of instrumental complexes." And it is this "existed" body which is the center of reference from which one finds oneself in the midst of beings and as an actual or possible being for others. The individual's contingent and concrete existence in the world for consciousness is revealed through the facticity of the body.

The individual, as consciousness-body, acts in relation to instrumental things which are perceived as figures upon the ground of the world. This world is construed as a totality and, by implication, a totality in process. The self, too, is described as a totality in the world and, as striving to realize specific possibilities, a "detotalized totality." What Sartre seems to mean by this phrase is that the individual, as transcending towards a variety of possibilities, is not a stable or enduring totality, but a dynamic totality. Needless to say, this phenomenological terminology will be preserved in the *Critique de la raison dialectique,* but given a slightly different application.

The so-called "choice" of the world which Sartre describes refers specifically to the apprehension of its meaning and, by implication, the meaning of objects encountered in the world. A conscious engagement in an action (or endeavor to realize a project) is something which must be intentionally sustained by a choice or decision which is an expression of "ex-

---

27. *Ibid.*, p. 371.
28. *Ibid.*, p. 381.

istential freedom." That is, despite the obstacles one encounters in an action (e.g., climbing a mountain, crossing a river, driving a truckload of equipment, etc.) one presumably chooses to yield to fatigue, to rest, to abandon the project. The negation of the fulfilment of a given project is always, in Sartre's view, theoretically possible. What this negation implies is "a radical conversion of my being-in-the world." Sartre desires, at all costs, to preserve the notion of our responsibility for our sustained project or its abandonment; in effect, he is concerned to emphasize man's responsibility for his actions and for the way in which he construes his being in the world.

This basic responsibility of man as originator and sustainer of his projects and of his way of understanding his being-in-the-world will be characteristically exaggerated by Sartre to include a gratuitous "global" responsibility. Even he himself is not entirely faithful to the notion that it is man's "original choice" which "arranges the world with its meaning, its instrumental-complexes and its coefficient of adversity."[29] That is to say that his phenomenology of "doing" *(faire)* or action leads him into an ambiguous terrain in which the complete or apodictic clarity of what is, as it were, constituted by the act of choice of the consciousness-body or what is an element in the objective structure of the world (which, at one point, he describes as the "totality of the in-itself") seems no longer attainable.

Insofar as human reality is described as action *(être pour elle [realité-humaine] c'est agir)*, and insofar as it is said that consciousness cannot exist without a given or "exists in terms of the given," action involves the engagement of consciousness in relation to the given. This is a crucial point in Sartre's ontology given the previous emphases upon the radical distinction between consciousness and its opposite. For, in his description of "the relation of freedom to facticity" *(des rapports de la liberté a la facticité)* Sartre considers what he calls the "reverse side" of freedom, the shift from abstract to concrete freedom, from what may be called the negative, ideal freedom of consciousness to man's actual freedom as circumscribed by "limitations."

The reversed perspective indicated here is reminiscent of Hegel's description of the observation of self-consciousness in its pure form and in its relation to the external. For, Hegel describes "acting consciousness which exists for itself" as engaged in canceling otherness and, in this reflexive awareness, finding its reality "in this direct awareness of itself as the negative."[30] The influences of the external circumstances or the exteriority

---

29. *Ibid.*, p. 53.
30. G. W. F. Hegel, *The Phenomenology of Mind*, trans. J. B. Baillie, London, 1931, p. 331.

of facticity is referred back to "formal consciousness." A world for an individual, as Hegel puts it, has a double meaning insofar as it is what it is in itself and it is the world for the individual. Sartre's account of freedom in situation has the basic form of Hegel's phenomenology of this stage of spiritual development. On the one hand, there is the "external circumstance completely encompassing, circumscribing, and conditioning the individual"; on the other hand, the same phenomena are "translated into the form in which those circumstances are in the conscious individual."[31]

For Hegel, as well as Sartre, the world is in relation to individual consciousness in the sense that "the given" is "transformed and transmuted by the individual." The specificity of *what* will influence an individual depends entirely on individual consciousness itself.[32] The implicit paradox in Sartre's conception of concrete freedom in the world is that he retains the idealistic notion of the referential nature of the world, facticity, meaning and structure while also insisting upon the independent actuality of the in-itself which is now considered as encompassed in his notion of "the world." The world which is "chosen" by virtue of a projection toward a possible is not "its contexture as in-itself, but its meaning."[33] But the question is, what kind of precise relationship between the for-itself *qua* body and the apparently objective features of the world is possible?

Most of the concessions Sartre grants to the limitations on man's freedom for common sense will recur in his phenomenology of the relationship between individual action and society construed as a "totality in process" or a totality immanent in, and intimately related to, the totality of the world as a system of instrumental complexes. That is, that man is born into a set of already constituted situations: he is born into this class rather than another, in this nation, or is born with these specific hereditary or congenital dispositions, features, or physiological characteristics. And Sartre seems to admit, without his usual proviso about the "choice" of this or that way of construing the world, that "the coefficient of adversity of things is such that years of patience are necessary to obtain the feeblest result."[34] From the common sense point of view (which Sartre recognizes, but repudiates), man seems more "to be made" than "to make himself." In his *Critique* Sartre will acknowledge the efficacy of the determination of our individuality in terms of causal factors without abandoning the general notions that the world and the specific structures or things in it are *for* con-

---

31. *Ibid.*, p. 335.
32. *Ibid.*, p. 334.
33. J. P. Sartre, *L'Être et le néant*, p. 541.
34. *Ibid.*, p. 561.

sciousness and the conception of action in terms of a transcendence towards a posited end or finality.

It is argued — against common sense — that the apparently objective "coefficient of adversity in things" has its reality only in reference to an individual's posited projects. The *soi-disant* brute existents which limit man's concrete freedom are ostensibly referential to our freedom itself insofar as it "must first constitute the framework, the technique, and the ends in relation to which they will manifest themselves as limits." It may be said, then, that all (apparent) negation of our concrete freedom is determined by that freedom itself. But Sartre is compelled by his own ontology to admit the residual actuality of the in-itself. He endeavors to obviate this necessary ingredient in the world by arguing that freedom *can only be freedom* in relation to the being of "brute existents." In what amounts to a sublation of his previous description of the negative freedom of consciousness in its own nihilating activity, Sartre now suggests that the freedom of consciousness as "nothingness" is ethereal, abstract, purely theoretical. If there were only the freedom of abstract, isolated consciousness, then the world would be a perpetual dream in which the conceptual, the imaginary, and the actual would be indistinguishable; or, as Sartre puts it, the possible and the real (or actual) would be indistinguishable. Now, it would seem, the only way in which the in-itself could be "negated" (or, more modestly, transformed or modified) is by means of the concrete free action of an individualized consciousness-body or self. From this reversed perspective, Sartre now insists that:

> ... the very order of the existents is indispensable to freedom itself. It is by means of them that freedom ... makes known to it what it is. Consequently the resistance which freedom reveals in the existent, far from being a danger to freedom, results only in enabling it to arise as freedom. There can be a free for-itself only as engaged in a resisting world.[35]

Concrete human freedom is conceived of as the "autonomy of choice" in relation to a resistant world that is actual and independent (in its being, if not in its meaning or form) of consciousness. Sartre fully realizes that his phenomenology of concrete, free action is a double-edged sword insofar as he has been led to admit that man's freedom does encounter limitations which are immanent in "the given" and which it endeavors to surpass. That the coefficient of adversity in things is encountered as an *obstacle* seems to entail the notion that, *malgré lui*, Sartre had been led to admit "something like an ontological conditioning of freedom" (*un conditionnement ontologique de la liberté*). For, he is unwilling to hold that human

---

35. *Ibid.*, p. 563.

freedom "creates its own obstacle." In actuality, man's freedom is self-determining in "doing" something to or with something and implies a relation to the given. But, once again, Sartre withdraws from the implications of his analysis by affirming that "the given" presumably cannot, in any way, "constitute" individual freedom. However, in one sense, what is given does constitute human freedom to the extent that its actual obstacles limit that freedom. To be sure, this is a limited constitution of freedom and not a complete constitution of it. It is clear that the lines of constitution or determination tend to intersect as Sartre's analysis leads him to the point of concretely relating consciousness and encountered facticity ("brute existents"). Even though one may grant that "the world by coefficients of adversity reveals to me the way in which I stand in relation to the ends which I assign myself," it is obvious that the distinction between what emerges from man's freedom and what emerges through the presence of exteriority is no longer easy to make. Sartre's own admission of this suggests a dialectical interrelationship between concrete freedom expressed in action (or *praxis*) and the obstacles encountered in the field of freedom.

That it is admitted that:

> ... the *situation,* the common product of the contingency of the in-itself and of freedom, is an ambiguous phenomenon in which it is impossible for the for-itself to distinguish the contribution of freedom from that of the brute existent ... [and that] it is impossible to decree *a priori* what comes from the brute existent and what comes from freedom in the character of this or that particular existent functioning as an obstacle,[36]

clearly indicates an implicit notion of the dialectical interplay of the world of non-conscious entities and concrete consciousness which finds its fulfillment in Sartre's description of the complex dialectic of social existence. Furthermore, the admission that situation is an "ambiguous phenomenon" suggests, in embryo, the process he will describe in the *Critique* as the interiorization of the exterior and the exteriorization of the interior. For, this formulation seems to be an endeavor to clarify what remains ambiguous in Sartre's earlier account of concrete action. The paradoxical nature of man's freedom discerned by Sartre in his ontology of the significant modes of being is incorporated into his dialectical analysis of the relations among men, groups and the material milieu of instrumental complexes. What Sartre says about the "paradox of freedom" is never abandoned in his later thought. That is, that:

> ... there is freedom only in a *situation,* and there is a situation only through freedom. Human reality everywhere encounters resistance and

---

36. *Ibid.,* p. 568.

obstacles which it has not created, but these resistances and obstacles have meaning only in and through . . . human reality.[37]

Despite Sartre's heroic (but unconvincing) attempt to show that our place, our environment, our past, our position, etc., are all referred back to human reality as such or to a "choice" of these facticities, his arguments seem to conflate the meaning of a facticity with its existence as part of one's biography. To be sure, the causal factors which condition the emergence of my individuality may be "chosen" retrospectively (as in the case of Kierkegaard's notion of "choosing oneself" in the sense that one accepts the causal factors influencing one's past and appropriates them as aspects of one's self), but this does not mean that I am free to choose the nation into which I am born, free to choose the natural language I have been taught, or free to choose my bodily characteristics. Granted that freedom enables me to reveal the facticities of my existence, it is questionable to refer these contingent facticities to any choice whatsoever. One's concrete facticity is subject to interpretation and the meaning-bestowing activity of consciousness; but, as significant elements in our life-history, such facticities are insurpassable empirical conditions of our life. That Sartre is on slippery ground in his analysis of such facticities is clear in his contradiction of his previous assertions. For, in the midst of endeavoring to make man responsible, in some way, for the fundamental facticities of his existence, he remarks that "our freedom itself creates the obstacles from which we suffer."[38] This is diametrically opposed to his previous standpoint and it indicates that he has had to reverse his previous understanding of facticity in order to make this far weaker analysis work. That it doesn't work is made clear by what he is willing to admit. Thus, *en passant,* he mentions that there are *some* unchangeable elements in one's past (e.g., an illness in childhood) which presumably are not freely "chosen." But it would seem that if some events in one's past are independent, unalterable actualities, would we not suspect that there are a multiplicity of similar events in one's life-history? To be sure, it can be granted that the meaning of any specific event in one's past is a matter of constitutive interpretation in relation to the "totality of my being." But this does not entail a denial of the sequence of objective, verifiable factual events in my past. It is simply absurd to argue, for example, that in being born I take a place for which I am

---

37. *Ibid.*, p. 569-570.
38. *Ibid.*, p. 576: "Ainsi la liberté crée elle-meme les obstacles dont nous souffrons."

responsible.[39] That the facticities in our lives are "discovered" through freedom does not mean that they are, in some mysterious fashion, chosen by virtue of individual freedom. I do not confer existence upon an actual event which occurred in the past when I determine its meaning for me in relation to present projects.

Sartre insists that "freedom is the apprehension of my facticity" even though he had admitted that it is sometimes difficult to distinguish in situation what is given in facticity and what is contributed by freedom. It would seem that a similar ambiguity would be encountered in an understanding of our own facticity. It is clear, at any rate, that there is a reciprocal relationship between facticity and freedom insofar as "freedom would not exist" without facticity and facticity is only discovered as meaningful through freedom. This relationship has a fundamental validity. But Sartre's exaggerations about the "dependence" of facticity on "freedom" are often based upon a theoretical fragility which, at times, he himself seems to recognize. This is especially the case in his attempt to show that it is human freedom which chooses "the meanings" already constituted (*déjà constituée*) by others in a society, a nation or a civilization, including the meanings conveyed through the medium of a natural language.

While admitting that one discloses not only an individual world (a world for subjective consciousness) but finds oneself in "an already meaningful world" sustained by a multiplicity of others, he must show that even these meanings expressed as "a strictly human coefficient of adversity" are freely chosen by the individual. Since individuals do not generate the evolution of a language (which is construed as a technique for apprehending meaning in the world), and since "the for-itself" has not created "these linguistic organizations or techniques," it would seem that here we have uncovered an insurpassable system of meanings which limit our freedom. Sartre appears to acknowledge this when he avers that:

> We should not think of denying this fact. For that matter our problem is not to show that the for-itself is the free foundation of its being; the for-

---

39. *Ibid.*, In *Sartre: A Philosophic Study*, (New York, 1967), Anthony Manser seems to me to be over-generous with Sartre's view while suggesting some reservations about his arguments in this context. He avers, that "the situation of an individual is his finitude, the starting-point . . . for any free action . . . Even that most arbitrary of all aspects of life, birth itself, is something which the individual chooses, in the sense that this does not limit his metaphysical freedom. Everyone who exists has to have been born, and this implies born of particular parents at a particular time and place. Birth is not a limitation, but, like the other aspects of the situation, a condition of freedom . . . Sartre's argument here is complex, and seems to involve . . . changing the meaning of the key terms involved . . . Sartre is making a point which needs making, though it may well be that it ought not to be expressed in terms of 'freedom.' [p. 133].

itself is free but *in condition*, and it is in the relation of this condition to freedom that we are trying to define by making clear the meaning of the situation."[40]

Despite this statement, Sartre repeats his usual arguments: we understand meaningful sentences because we recognize in such sentences the expression of the "movement" of the transcendence of the other; freedom is the only conceivable foundation of "the laws of language;" linguistic utterances are free projects of designation which issue from the personal choice of an individual consciousness; the use of a specific natural language is a free choice of consciousness, etc. All of Sartre's admissions about the techniques and meanings already sustained by other persons and encountered by an individual consciousness undermine his insistence upon the free projects of individuals which presumably enable an individual to "choose itself beyond certain meanings of which it is not the origin."[41] This ostensible transcendence is clearly illusory since individual consciousness expresses its freedom in a world already constituted, a world comprised of a referential system of meanings which make concrete freedom possible and meaningful. Sartre's attempt to obviate the undeniable, insurpassable conditioning influence of one's nationality, one's social status, and the natural language which one initially learns on one's concrete existence is not merely paradoxical, but simply unjustifiable. It is not merely that individual consciousness must "take account of these circumstances" for the very notions of a "for itself," a "consciousness," "human freedom," etc., are themselves expressions of meanings acquired by an individual and have emerged in the history of human thought.

To be sure, it is, as Sartre repeatedly says, in *this world* that freedom comes into play; but this world encompasses a multiplicity of causal factors that cannot be freely chosen by the subjective consciousness of an individual. Sartre seems to acknowledge this when he remarks that "to be free is not to choose the historic world in which one arises—which would have no meaning—but to choose oneself in the world whatever this may be."[42] The meanings encountered in the socio-historical world are, of course, capable of transformation, are subject to negation through theoretical or practical projects, and are not eternal. But as an individual emerges as a self-conscious person he has already been affected by a number of linguistic, theoretical, and practical meaning-structures which

---

40. *Ibid.*, p. 602.
41. *Ibid.*
42. *Ibid.*, p. 604: "Car être libre n'est pas choisir le monde historique où l'on surgit—ce qui n'aurait point de sens—mais se choisir dans le monde, quel qu'il soit."

are immanent in this unique individual's understanding of himself, others, non-conscious beings and the world in which he finds himself. In his various discussions of concrete freedom Sartre seems, at times, alternately to accept and to deny this. If human freedom is only truly meaningful in relation to particular factual structures, then there is freedom only in a socio-cultural context which is not arbitrarily chosen by an individual. The *situation* is, as Sartre points out, neither subjective nor objective. What is suggested by Sartre's analysis is that a concrete situation is a dialectical interaction, a dynamic synthesis, of consciousness and facticity. If he hesitates — in *Being and Nothingness* — to say this explicitly it is probably because of his desire to preserve a questionable notion of absolute freedom. But such a mode of freedom is possible, in Sartre's terms, only for the for-itself as abstract, isolated consciousness, a pure consciousness which is, in itself, nothing. Insofar as one is seriuosly considering actual, concrete, historical freedom, this notion of freedom remains a kind of ideality which must be renounced. If one wants one's action to have efficacy one must strive to realize one's projects in a actual field of beings-in-themselves and facticities and one must endeavor to overcome real obstacles, real limitations upon one's freedom. If man creates himself, he does so in terms of factual limitations on his capacities (rooted in the past), and in relation to independently existing facticities; his finitude — which Sartre recognizes — is precisely the ultimate limitation on his self-creating activity. Consciousness may be said to "illuminate" a situation, to render it meaningful; but it does not create concrete situations. In the *Critique de la raison dialectique* Sartre will come to acknowledge factual determinations or limitations without introducing the proviso of an ideal freedom. In addition, the dialectical relationship between individual consciousness and the world as a system of instrumental complexes (which, I believe, is implicit in *Being and Nothingness)* will become a central focus of concern for Sartre. Before turning to this question, we must consider another significant modality of being of "human reality" which has important ramifications for a theory of social reality — that is, being-for-others.

II. FREEDOM AND EXISTENCE FOR OTHERS

> "... the other is also a self-consciousness; an individual makes its appearance in antithesis to an individual."
>
> G. W. F. Hegel, *The Phenomenology of Mind*

The descriptions of the world for consciousness already suggested the possible or actual encounter with others who exist in a complex social milieu in which there are systems of signification and reference which attest to shared meanings. The impenetrable being-in-itself is not the only entity which is independent of individual consciousness. For, there is the world of persons and their bodies which is both *for* consciousness and a facticity encountered in one's being-in-the-world. Each individual finds himself, as a reflective being, in a world possessing meanings which have been created by others. The other is the ultimate "center of reference" for these transmitted meanings or what Dilthey would call "expressions of life." The presence of other people in the world is attested to not only by our perception of their bodies as 'objects' in the world, but by the sense of our "existence-in-the-presence-of-others" *(l'existence-dans-le-monde-en-presence-d'autres)*. How others are understood or 'seen' is said to be based upon an individual's choice; that is, one presumably chooses to view the other as object or as subject. These alternative ways of thinking of other persons are the determining factors influencing *how* we experience others in social relations.

It is no secret that, generally speaking, Sartre adopts a strikingly pessimistic interpretation of our typical relationships with others. While he may not completely share the view of his character in *No Exit (Huis clos)* that "Hell is other people," he does describe the relations between man and man as permeated by an underlying or overt hostility. This conception of human relationships will find its way into his *Critique* insofar as "the other" is described there as a perpetual threat, containing in himself the possibility of my own negation. It is as if Sartre merely projects his phenomenological psychology of being-for-others onto the larger canvases of history and social reality. However, the spiritual conflict between individual consciousness which is described in *Being and Nothingness* more or less along the lines of Hegel's phenomenology of the "master-slave" relationship is given a material basis in the *Critique* which serves only to intensify the antagonism between man and man in the Sartrean world. It is clear that the dialectical network of interrelationships amongst individuals (and groups) presented in his social phenomenology is merely an amplification and refinement of Sartre's psychological analysis of the *dialectical* relationships between individual consciousness and others. The reciprocal relationships of determination and negation, exteriority and interiority, the mutual recognitions of each other in the interplay between the subjective individual and the other reappear in Sartre's later work in his description of the social dialectic. In regard to this aspect of Sartre's thought the continuity between the earlier general ontology and the later social phenomenology is clearly discernible.

Existence for Others

Although Sartre repeatedly refers to *my* consciousness, *my* intentional projects, *my* possibilities, *my* being-in-the-world and *my* nihilating acts of consciousness, one suspects that all along he is, by implication, suggesting that what is characteristic of a subjective consciousness is, *mutatis mutandis,* characteristic of any human consciousness. The internal negations of consciousness as described in the analysis of "the immediate structure of the for-itself" already seem to imply a recognition of others either in their presence *for* consciousness or in their absence ("Pierre is not in the café."). In Sartre's description of *mauvaise foi* or "bad faith" he describes the inauthentic state of a person who flees from responsibility (and anguish in the face of possibility) for what he is and endeavors to become like an "in-itself" or to see himself as the other. Although Sartre insists that our immediate relation to others reveals them as objects in the world and, hence, as resembling beings-in-themselves, his entire phenomenology of the structure of consciousness seems to presuppose an intuitive recognition of the other as a personal being-for-itself. In this regard, he intends to avoid scrupulously the "reef of solipsism." Insofar as he is successful in doing so, he must rely upon an overt expression of the interiority of the other, that is, the "look" or "glance" *(le regard).* But even independent of the way in which the other reveals to me his consciousness by "fixing" me in his gaze (i.e., determining me in my facticity as an object), Sartre indicates that there is a fundamental recognition of the other as a human "object." For, in what he describes as the "intersubjectivity of the for-others" we are aware of "the alienating reality of the other" as possessing a consciousness which is inaccessible to us. Just as we are a "meaningful object" for the other, we may assume that the other is invariably a "meaningful object" for us.¹ Although Sartre sometimes suggests that the other is experienced concretely as if it were an "in-itself," he is not always consistent in this regard insofar as he implicitly incorporates into his analysis of others the apprehension of a humanized object. That is, in our initial relationship to others, we never experience them in a social world as indistinguishable from the massive, inert being-in-itself which circumscribes our consciousness. Insofar as I recognize the other as a bodily "being-in-itself," I simultaneously realize that this "presence" to my consciousness — as a *body* — "belongs to the totality which we call "human reality" as one of its structures."²

The significant characteristic of my encounter with others is the mutual, reciprocal relationship of negation: in recognizing the other, the other is determined as an object while one's own recognition by the other is a determination of oneself as an object for the field of consciousness of the other. Although Sartre tends to deny that this reciprocal relationship is dialectical, his description of this interaction between individual consciousness and the other is clearly dialectical in its form. This is obviously the case in Sartre's description of the "unrealizable ideal" of unification with the other which is a fundamental source of conflict. For, the process of reciprocal relationship is characterized by my experience of myself as an object for the other and my project of assimilating the other through this experience. Since the other views me as an object in the world (and does not, in fact, project identifying himself with me), "being-for-others" entails a dual internal negation insofar as one would seek to act upon "the internal negation by which the Other transcends my transcendence."³ Even if such an endeavor to act upon the freedom of another is doomed to failure, the entire process is clearly dialectical (*pace* Sartre's denials).

Precisely in the very recognition of oneself as transcending the transcendence of others one sees oneself in a social milieu which is quite different from our immediate experience of beings-in-themselves in a world. If, as Sartre says, "in the recognition of my object-state [I] have proof that he [the other] has this consciousness,"⁴ then it is also the case that I know that I am an object-for-others which is meaningful and already

---

1. J. P. Sartre, *L'Être et le néant*, p. 442: ". . .´. pour l'autre, je demeure objet significant — ce que j'ai toujours été."
2. *Ibid.*, p. 278 " . . . le corps appartient à la totalité que nous nommons réalité humaine comme une de ses structures."
3. *Ibid.*, p. 433.
4. *Ibid.*, p. 431: "Et moi, dans la reconnaissance de mon objectité, j'eprouve qu'il a cette conscience."

humanized. For, one finds oneself in a world-milieu which is other than that of either an isolated consciousness or that of the inert in-itself. Sartre's entire analysis of the existence of others and my being for them reveals a social dimension of human relationships characterized by the interplay of individual consciousnesses and individual bodies. At this stage of his descriptive analysis Sartre no longer speaks of the world for *my* consciousness, but of the world in which I am an object for others and others are objects for me. Although he claims that the "we-world" *(wir-Welt)* Heidegger refers to in *Sein und Zeit* is a "secondary and subordinate experience" in relation to our original experience of the other, it seems to me that the "we-subject" recognition that is referred to is implicit in Sartre's phenomenology of our experience of others and their experience of us. In a sense, the so-called original experience which is described can be construed as the psychological basis for the apprehension of a larger social totality. But the latter is already implicit in the former.

The primordial relationship between consciousness and what it is not (including others) is, as Sartre insists, one of negation. In this sense, then, the negation of the other as a consciousness with its own unique projects and possibilities must be *prior* to the recognition of my existence as a bodily object for others. Sartre is already committed to the view that "positive realities" such as the bodies of others require negation in order that their sharp outlines be fixed. The apprehension of the body of the other requires, then, the nihilating activity of consciousness which Sartre describes in his analysis of the for-itself. Despite himself, however, Sartre avers (against his later description of the experience of others) that:

> ... the for-itself of the Other is not a hidden phenomenon which would be given only as the conclusion of a reasoning by analogy. It manifests itself originally to my for-itself.[5]

This implicit recognition of others as having a consciousness seems required by Sartre's notion that the apprehension of something as a determinate being is possible on the basis of the negation of something. Thus, in recognizing myself as other for another it is necessary, as it were, to negate myself as subjective consciousness. This is precisely how Sartre characterizes the possibility of recognizing myself as not the other and, hence, revealing the other *qua* other. That is,

> If in general there is an Other, it is necessary above all that I be the one who is not the Other, and it is in this very negation effected by me upon myself that I make myself be and that the Other arises as Other.[6]

---

5. *Ibid.*, p. 139.
6. *Ibid.*, p. 343.

By relating these two notions we can see that Sartre's description of the other person as a body practically requires a prior apprehension of others as human beings or persons. The dual "internal negation" of consciousness as not being this being (the other) and the negation of the "other —as— subject" are the necessary conditions for the recognition of the other as object. Sartre must hold that "our human-reality must . . . be simultaneously for-itself and for-others."[7] In non-Sartrean terms this means that all along we have recognized other people as objects *and* as subjects insofar as we clearly distinguish them from the impenetrable, massive inert in-itself in our ordinary, prephilosophical experience. If this is the case, then Sartre has implicitly acknowledged the social dimension of human experience in *Being and Nothingness* as a primary condition of human life. The social existence of man which seems to have been bracketed in the phenomenology of consciousness is an inescapable dimension of my being since, as Sartre admits, I find myself in a world of meanings, significations, organizations, institutions, etc., which my consciousness has not created and which are, at first, imposed upon me. That some apprehension of the exteriorization of other subjects has already placed a limit on my concrete freedom (if not the abstract freedom of isolated consciousness) is clear from Sartre's remark that:

> The Other is in no way given to us as an object . . . The objectivation of the Other . . . is a defense on the part of my being which, precisely by conferring on the Other a being-for-me frees me from my being-for-Others.[8]

Applying the kind of psychological analysis Sartre freely practices on others (Baudelaire, Flaubert, Genet, etc.) to himself, it seems that one of Sartre's fundamental deep-seated resentments (as revealed in the description of his childhood in *Les Mots*) is the power which society and significant others wield over the individual in his earliest stages of development, the sense of being formed and shaped by the values, desires, fantasies and needs of others. His early hyperbolic defense of subjective freedom can be seen as a reaction to these external determinations of one's self. And his analysis of others as threatening, negating, dangerous and destructive reveals this idiosyncratic understanding of the conditioning of the self by others. Although the other is said to contain within himself the "menace of death" in the *Critique* Sartre has, more or less, come to terms with the social actuality he seems to have avoided in *Being and Nothing-*

---

7. *Ibid.*, p. 342: "Sans doute notre réalité humaine exige-t-elle d'être simultanément pour-soi et pour autrui, mais nos recherches présentes ne visent pas a constituer une antropologie. "The *Critique* will be described by Sartre as precisely an anthropological study.
8. *Ibid.*, p. 327.

ness (perhaps for the reason I have suggested). For, in the *Critique,* the collectivity of other persons sharing a common interest, bond, value, or goal is now seen as a means of attaining greater individual freedom. But we shall see whether Sartre does, in fact, preserve individual freedom as an ultimate value in his social philosophy.

Returning to the details of his treatment of the existence of others we can discern a certain vacillation on precisely the question whether we first encounter other people as objects or whether we are not, *ab initio,* aware of the existence of others as body-consciousnesses in a social milieu. In his initial account of others Sartre notes that the appearance of others is primarily manifested by virtue of "organized forms such as gestures and expressions, acts and conduct."[9] There are, in fact, associated groups of phenomena discovered in my experience that attest to the existence of someone other than myself. These phenomena are described by Dilthey as "spiritual expressions of life" which are deemed manifestations of a *geistige Welt* which is other than the world of natural phenomena. Sartre argues that such phenomena suggest the existence of others on an "as if" basis until we have a direct experience of the other in his alterity.

What Sartre seems to mean here is that the discovery of "systems of meaning and experiences" which are quite distinct from my own suggests the independent existence of the other even though we do not know that the other exists until we directly experience his being for us and the simultaneous recognition of our being for others. There are, however, occasional lapses in his discussion of the sequences of experiences which lead us to the recognition of the other-as-object and the other-as-subject. For, at one point, he explicitly avers that "it is undeniable that the instrumental-thing (i.e., any object for use or what Heidegger calls a *zuhanden*) from the moment of its discovery refers to a plurality of For-itselfs."[10] This notion is closer to Dilthey's view that the discovery of a meaningful structure of any kind in the world presupposes the actual present or past existence of an individual person who has objectified his *Erlebnis* or "lived experience" in a phenomenon which is imprinted, as it were, with the purposive intentionality of man. In Sartre's later language we could say that we discover in systems of signification an exteriorization of the interiorization of human consciousness.

Insofar as we hold Sartre to such assertions, it is clear that the disclosure of the existence of the other is initially as characterized by the in-

---

9. *Ibid.,* p. 280.
10. *Ibid.,* p. 289: "Il est incontestable que la chose-utensile renvoie dès sa découverte à une pluralité de Pour-soi."

teriority of his consciousness which, of course, is never directly perceived or known by us. This notion tends to undermine his occasional emphasis upon the immediate experience of the other as a body or "pure exteriority" which is an "in-itself." The recognition of other people as having human expressions, as speaking a natural language, as acting in an apparently intentional way already seems to entail the recognition of others as consciousnesses insofar as the consciousness of "human reality" is rooted in situation through bodily existence. To be sure, the other seen as a bodily object is not the same as the other as aware of "existing" its bodily facticity "from within." The point is that Sartre's phenomenology of individual being seems to commit him to the view that the disclosure of a humanized object (a body) for my consciousness is accompanied by the well-founded belief that this body is "existed" by another consciousness.

In Sartre's account, the other is described as the mediator of my self-consciousness insofar as one becomes self-conscious (in terms of a Hegelian notion) only by means of the realization of my determination of the existence of the other and the other's determination of myself. As Sartre puts it, "the primary fact is the plurality of consciousness, and this plurality is realized in the form of a double, reciprocal relation of exclusion."[11] This process of "reciprocal imbrication" or overlapping of relationships indicates what I would consider as a prolepsis of Sartre's later notion of dialectical interrelations between the social individual and the other, one group and another. In the sense that Sartre maintains that one's self-consciousness is dependent on the other, the other is necessarily a limiting factor of my concrete freedom insofar as the mutual determination of oneself and the other presupposes a concrete encounter with another in a situation in which a significant aspect of my facticity (and that of the other) is revealed to me through the other. The encounter with others, then, may be construed as *the* determining factor of my facticity as being-in-the-world. The world in which one now finds oneself is clearly a social world despite the fact that Sartre presents his phenomenology of the other in abstraction from the milieu presupposed as the ground against which myself and others are discerned.

While we may be said to experience states of consciousness — fear, shame and pride — which imply a referential awareness of the existence of other individuals, we presumably encounter others as modifying our world through their presence not merely as threats to our existence, judges of our misbehavior or as courts of appeal for our aggrandizement. The enclave of other people is established through their behavior, their action. Such ac-

---

11. *Ibid.*, pp. 291-292.

tivity reveals the organizing function of the other as a "totality." The question is, is Sartre correct in assuming our immediate awareness of another is as an object for consciousness?

If it be granted that my casual glance at another human being is primarily an intentional, but non-thetic, awareness of an object occupying space or moving through space, this is by no means my only immediate apprehension of others. For, it is also the case that we often perceive others immediately in relation to their function or social role. Even the child (as soon as he or she is capable of speaking) tends to refer to that being as "a policeman" or "the postman" or a "teacher." The clerk in a store does not see a moving object approaching his counter; he sees a "customer." My immediate recognition of a person who is a doctor is not of a "bodily object," but "a doctor." To be sure, these commonplace identifications of others in terms of their particular function as perceived by me is, of course, impersonal. But it is, nevertheless, a common instance of *how* I experience an encounter with other people. In this sense, as I've suggested, Sartre's earlier description of our sense of the existence of others seems to bracket, in a gratuitous fashion, our seeing others in a social context. For most of our lives the majority of our immediate encounters with other people are impersonal relationships in which we identify the other with their social function or social role. To ignore this immediate mode of being for a consciousness in a phenomenology of our apprehension of others is to ignore a significant dimension of the "alienating reality of others." Needless to say, Sartre places proper emphasis upon this specific kind of apprehension of others in his *Critique de la raison dialectique*. To my mind, its deemphasis in *Being and Nothingness* is a serious lacuna in his description of how we immediately see others.

The subsequent analysis of our experience of others as subjects who, nevertheless, elude us as subjects, is a significant factor in the determination of our factical limitations. It is to be noted that, in this connection, Sartre does not say anything about our *choosing* this mode of our facticity. The presence of the "strange freedom" of others may, paradigmatically, be expressed through the "look" or *regard,* but it is also experienced in any number of different ways. Gestures of friendliness or hostility can have more or less the same function. Indeed, the speech of others (from which distinctive, individuating voiceprints can be made) serves to reveal to me not only their impersonal otherness, but their otherness as subjects. In point of fact, all concentrated activities (tying a knot, performing surgery, driving an automobile) tend to lead us to ascribe states of consciousness to such agents (as P. F. Strawson points out in *Individuals*). While the case of animal behavior is admittedly obscure and subject to the fallacy of anthropomorphism, it seems perfectly plausible for us to ascribe intentionality and purposiveness to other beings who resemble ourselves. *Le regard* or "the look" is only one instance in which others reveal themselves to us as conscious subjects who are capable of fixing us in our facticity for them. The quality of the "sculpturing" of myself as an object for others is somewhat obscure in Sartre's early phenomenology insofar as he claims that the certitude of the existence of the other is independent of my specific experiences. This is paradoxical, to say the least, since it is solely through my individual, specific experiences of others that I come to believe that there are others. Furthermore, the supplementary notion that the other-as-subject is a "prenumerical reality,"[12] a Heideggerian "one" *(das Man)* is simply obscure. To be sure, the fact that (to take Sartre's example) Genet is "looked at" and is thereby fixed in his facticity as a "thief" by a particular individual is a purely contingent factor since anyone could have "caught him in the act." But, from a phenomenological standpoint, the other who reveals himself as a subject through, say, a scornful look is always *one* and this particular individual. This is clear in an instance when one is caught in an embarrassing situation by (a) an anonymous other, and (b) another person whose opinion and judgement one respects. In the latter case we may assume a more intense embarrassment which indicates the relevance of the particular other whom one encounters unexpectedly. In addition, the distinctive form or mode of the look of the other may be clearly individuated in any given instance. The point I want to make is that Sartre's generalization about the implicative relation between myself and the other as involving my being the other in general for someone else does not stand up to analysis. Nor is it necessarily always the case that the other, prior to my objectification of him, is merely a "prenumerical one." My being apprehended by another is also both an impersonal determination of myself and, quite often, an individuating one. Just as I am sometimes capable of providing rather detailed descriptions of the individual characteristics of others, so, too, it may legitimately be assumed that others can do the same in my case.

The reciprocal relationship between an individual and the other requires, for Sartre, a negation of the other in order to be myself and presupposes a negation of my consciousness by the other.[13] Invariably, the other being is given not only as a body but is granted an inferred subjectivity. What this means, in effect, is that there is a reciprocal, dialectical process of constitution which is fundamentally experienced as a tension between

---

12. *Ibid.*, p. 341ff.
13. *Ibid.*, p. 435.

two individuals. This notion of conflict and tension between oneself and the other is a fundamental notion in Sartre's thought which finds its continuing expression in the conflict between man and man in social relations. Sartre seems blind to the actual relationships of love, friendship, and cooperation amongst individuals which are fundamentally based upon a suspension or negation of what often does appear to be a mutually excluding relationship between one self and another. What I am suggesting is that there may very well be some substance to Sartre's account of many *impersonal* encounters between man and man even though there are some personal human relationships which put this primitive conflicting relationship out of action. Surely, it is not the case that I must "possess" the subjectivity of the other in order to complete the circle of love. In all probability, love, trust, friendship and cooperation would be far less prevalent in human relationships if each person had complete access to the subjective interiority of the other. Sartre, *malgré lui,* seems fascinated by Hegel's model of the "master-slave" relationship and seems to have been unable to transcend this dramatic model of the encounter of self with the other self.

Social Dimensions of the Other

What Sartre describes as the "upsurge" of the other in my world seems to entail the simultaneous constitution of interpersonal meanings within a spatial social field in which there is some indirect comprehension of the projects or purposes of others.[14] Insofar as being-for-others is an ontological relationship there are a plurality of subjects which are interconnected by virtue of a *nexus* of being. The unity of the relationships amongst subjective consciousness and others is presupposed in Sartre's account from the hypothetical perspective of a "third" person observing this complex process. But the perspective disclosing the totality of the relationship between consciousness and others is not attainable in terms of a concrete description of the immanent encounter of consciousness and the other. Although "my freedom is alienated in the presence of the Other's pure subjectivity which founds my objectivity,"[15] the totality of the dual alienation is not disclosed in the concrete reciprocal relationships themselves except by the introduction of a hypothetical third person. This introduction of "the third" is clearly the ontological foundation for the complex network of reciprocal relationships amongst men in a social, and

---

14. Cf. A. Schuetz, "Sartre's Theory of the Alter Ego," *Philosophy and Phenomenological Research,* IX, p. 197ff.
15. J. P. Sartre, *op. cit.,* p. 443.

not only psychological, context which is foreshadowed in *Being and Nothingness*.

By moving from a discussion of a pair of individuals encountering each other in a kind of theoretical isolation to a consideration of a situation in which this antagonistic relationship takes place in relationship to a multiplicity of others, Sartre introduces the notion of a communal existence which had hitherto been bracketed in order to discern through phenomenological description the essential features of the experience of the existence of the other. This latter discussion has been clearly an abstract analysis which lacked the social context in which such encounters actually take place. When "the third" *(le Tiers)* individual is considered one experiences these others as "forming a community."[16] That is, I experience the "we-as-subject" which is an indeterminate situation which is subject to metastasization. The other is now discovered as an object in the midst of the world of a multiplicity of "thirds." In simple terms, the world of a society is disclosed. For, we now encounter a situation in the world in which oneself and the other may be understood as *"equivalent* structures in *solidarity* with each other."[17] That is to say that one discovers oneself as related to another (or a group of others) in terms of a solidarity which had formerly not been experienced. Now one experiences oneself as belonging to a loosely structured totality which Sartre describes as "them" insofar as myself and the other have, for "the third", a "meaning-for-others." Although this is ostensibly an alienating experience, it is clearly yet another determination of my facticity and an implicit limitation of my concrete freedom. For, one has not chosen to be associated with the other in a kind of loosely structured solidarity. Rather, it is a situation imposed from without by another person. As Sartre describes it in his somewhat dramatic language, "the one who experiences himself as constituting an *Us* with other men feels himself trapped among an infinity of strange existences."[18] Sartre regards this recognition of ourselves as an "us-object" as a subordinate modality of being-for-others. As such, however, it is one which will be the basis upon which he will found his phenomenology of group-formations. And, as I shall attempt to indicate, the description of this modality of human facticity is — in *Being and Nothingness* — more or less an anticipation of his later analysis of loosely structured social units (i.e., serialities) in the *Critique*.

We have seen thus far that the account of the relation between sub-

---

16. *Ibid.*, p. 487.
17. *Ibid.*, p. 489.
18. *Ibid.*, p. 491.

jective consciousness and the other has revealed a relationship which is, in a significant sense, quite different from the encounter of a consciousness with the in-itself. For, Sartre's analysis of the experience of others introduces a dual perspective which is absent from his description of the for-itself or consciousness. The description of others is characterized by the apprehension of an objective ontological perspective and a subjective orientation made manifest in his phenomenology of alterity or "otherness." In the description of the relationship between ego and alter-ego, the other is given to one from a subjective perspective and an objective ontological account of the alter-ego cannot evade an implicit understanding of the other as subject. This means that the dual process of reciprocal objectification of subjective consciousness and the other is clearly unlike the relationship between consciousness and the in-itself as an objective being which is wholly unlike consciousness itself. In Sartre's account, consciousness is engaged in a limitative relationship to the other. Now, the being-for-itself of human consciousness is characterized by an indirect reference to the other which suggests a dialectical interplay. As has recently been said:

> . . . being-for-others permits a dialectic on the lines of the previous analyses of the for-itself . . . This dialectic accordingly *construes* the alternating reciprocity of the encounter . . . As a result of Sartre's dialectic, being-for-others stands for a concrete foundation of the encounter as well as for a basic structure of the for-itself as such.[19]

In the primary phenomenology of other persons, each subjective consciousness is affected by its determination as an object by the other insofar as I am simultaneously aware that I am an object for an inaccessible consciousness. This is the basis for the conflict model which Sartre adopts in his understanding of the experience of others and the experience of being-for-others. Certainly there cannot be a similar mode of conflict in man's relationship to concrete obstacles encountered in situation. In this sense, the situation in which man is related to man has a unique ontological form which is other than any other kind of relationship between subjective consciousness and what it is not. Dual subjective orientations bring about in Sartre's ontology a paradoxical dialectic of reciprocal opposition which Sartre believes is never completely abrogated in man's social existence. One invariably encounters the other — at least initially — in an antithetical relationship which can, in cooperative endeavors, be mitigated or "bracketed," but never entirely overcome. In *Being and Nothingness,* even the associations amongst men, the positive social relations, are experienced as alienating. Despite this negativistic understanding of human associa-

---

19. Klaus Hartmann, *Sartre's Ontology,* p. 124.

tion, there are a number of themes expressed in Sartre's description of the "us-object" and the "we-subject" which are clear indications of the possible extension of his ontology into the domain of social reality. The schema of the social facticity of human existence in *Being and Nothingness* is a miniature which is obviously the model for the later larger portrait of the lived dialectic of human experience in a socio-cultural context.

The multiplicity of perceived human bodies presupposes a multiplicity of alter-egos intent upon realizing their projects in a world which is now clearly a world of instrumental complexes and of persons. The appearance of a third person is the condition for the possibility of a dual objectification of myself and others which generates a situation in which a purely human coefficient of adversity is disclosed. What Sartre calls the "world of the third" is clearly a *social* world. The third person, by defining myself and another, is the basis for seeing ourselves as together with the other in a more encompassing totality which, of course, I am precluded from seeing as a totality because of my immanence in it and because I lack the perspective of an ideal being-in-and-for-itself or God. The experience of being with others is paradigmatically revealed in "communal work", or in a situation in which there is a common productive activity requiring collective action which is apprehended by "the third." In what is obviously an anticipation of the language of the *Critique* he remarks that in a group engaged in some productive activity we apprehend ourselves:

. . . as an "us" *across* a material object "to be created." Materiality puts its seal on our solid community, and we appear to ourselves as an instrumental disposition and technique of means, each one having a particular place assigned by an end.[20]

The complex of meanings apprehended in such a situation is sustained by what is here a common project, a common goal as well as by the existence of the other person ("the third") who oversees this mutual engagement of individuals whose functions serve a common finality. In this description, it is now the third person who transcends others through his freedom. What Sartre applies to concrete individual action in situation is here transferred to group action insofar as such a "collectivity" can transcend intramundane objects in order to achieve its goals. In order that there be collective action of a collectivity in its own interests (e.g., to overcome a low standard of living), what is required is precisely what will be required for group action in the *Critique* — that is, a "common ideal". As is the case in his later conception of group formation, Sartre avers that the mere existence of a "privation" is insufficient for social unification insofar as a

---

20. J. P. Sartre, *op. cit.*, p. 491.

group does not see itself (or constitute itself) *as* a group. Privations in themselves tend to isolate men and they do not, by any means, "possess the possibility of unifying and of making each one assume the responsibility for the unification."[21] This association of individuals determined in their being by a third person and subject to privations which are experienced individually even though such individuals do discover themselves as an association will be the basic model for Sartre's concept of a diffuse social assembly which he describes as a seriality *(serialité)*. Or, more accurately, he will use this description of associations as the basis for a more general conception of any loosely structured assembly of people.

It is the presence of the third man which, for Sartre, is presumably the foundation for communal relationships amongst men insofar as he claims that, in the absence of "the third man," one would understand oneself as a "triumphant transcendence." This is an exaggeration in his own terms since he has already admitted that the existence of the other is a limitation on my freedom since I am not free from the determination of myself as an object for the other. The objectification of myself by another is only exacerbated by the existence of a third person or a host of third persons. The continuity of his description of being-for-others and this new mode of being in association with others seems to be affirmed by Sartre's remark that "the experience of the Us-object presupposes that of the being-for-others, of which it is only a more complex modality."[22] Although Sartre denies it, I believe that his description of the "we-subject" in his analysis of our concrete relations with others is also yet another modality of our being-for-others. That this is actually the case is suggested by Sartre himself in his observation that, in strongly structured groups, there is no longer only the project of expressing our freedom from the "us" by a reassertion of our individual existence, but an emerging project of liberating the entire group from an objectified state by a transformation of this assembly into a "we-subject."

Since such a project is freely chosen by an individual in a situation dominated by a sense of associative relationship which is itself a complex modality of being-for-others, there is no reason to believe that this new way of apprehending the possibilities emerging in a concrete situation is not also a residual extension of our being-for-others in a world of instrumental objects. The sustained sense of our being part of an assembly is supported by the fact that "in terms of *le regard* . . . we assume ourselves as Us" for

---

21. *Ibid.*, p. 492.
22. *Ibid.*, p. 493: ". . . c'est que l'épreuve du nos-objet suppose celle de l'être-pour-autrui dont elle n'est qu'une modalité plus complexe."

others. Although Sartre describes the project of realizing a complete "totalization" of individual consciousness and *all* others as impossible, he does indicate that the sense of an ideal "humanistic" community of all men is one possible (theoretically possible) extension of the more typical sense of the "us-object." What Sartre does not say is that it is, in terms of previous and subsequent analyses, the ineluctable coefficient of adversity of things and the conflict between man and man which makes this project of a unified humanity a quixotic ideal. It is Sartre's understanding of subjective consciousness, the obstacles encountered in concrete action, and his phenomenology of human relationships which prohibits him from projecting the goal of a humanistic world of cooperative action. Moreover, he goes so far as to say that the recovery of the "human totality" (i.e., the "humanistic Us") is only possible on the basis of positing the existence of a transcendent "third"—that is, God. In the absence of God, it is arbitrarily assumed that "the effort to realize humanity as *ours* is forever renewed and forever results in failure."[24] This peculiar notion (for a philosopher who describes himself as a humanist) is rooted in his pessimistic vision of the human world and is ultimately a natural consequence of Sartre's phenomenology of our being-for-others and their being-for-us. If there is a "conversion" in Sartre, it is from this negative vision of the utter hopelessness of a concrete humanism to the reconsideration of this possibility if "scarcity" is eliminated from the world. But even in the *Critique* it is still suggested that the goal of a humanistic social world is a remote possibility in a world that seems, by its very nature, to generate anti-dialectical forces, counterfinalities, and a host of *négatités*.

The transition to a discussion of the possibility of being "we-subjects" is announced by an assertion which seems paradoxical in light of previous analyses. It is said that it is the world itself which makes known to us our condition of being members of a "subject-community" and especially the actual existence of objects produced for use. Here, we must remind Sartre that he had argued repeatedly that the being of the world is "created" by consciousness and that a world, as Sartre understands it, is a complex network of instrumental objects. What is lacking here is the obvious interconnection between the apprehension of a world as comprised of instrumental complexes *and* others. For, the disclosure of others-as-objects is explicitly described as the discernment of particular relations which stand out in relief like figures on the ground of the world. Being-in-the-world must include a simultaneous awareness of utensils and others as objects juxtaposed

---

23. *Ibid.*, pp. 493-494.
24. *Ibid.*, p. 495.

to, or moving around and within, instrumental complexes. We know we belong to a "subject-community," even if we do not feel this communal relationship, insofar as we recognize manifestations of human significations in the world. The system of meanings disclosed in the world for consciousness already attests to the activity of human reality and, hence, to our involvement in a world already humanized. Paraphrasing Heidegger in *Sein und Zeit* we may say that there is no world without man and no men without a world. Knowledge of being-in-a-world and knowledge of belonging to a "subject-community" are, even in Sartre's terms, inseparable. The "objects . . . worked on by men" (the "worked upon matter" of the *Critique*) are immediately recognized as human creations. Existence in the world already discloses this existence as being in the presence of others who have already constituted a communal world in which there are techniques, instruments and significations which attest to the action or conduct of others as "transcendence-transcended." Consciousness discovers itself in the midst of these systems of meanings which it itself did not create and hence the facticity of the self in situation is always necessarily manifested in a human world or a humanized world. For Sartre, "there is no non-human situation."[25]

When Sartre asserts in the *Critique* that *dans l'univers toute existence est matérielle, [et] dans le monde de l'homme tout est humain,* he is, more or less, expressing a notion present in *Being and Nothingness:* that is, that the significant world in which man can exercise his limited *concrete* freedom is a humanized world, a world transformed and shaped by human action. What is surprising is his unwillingness to admit that our sense of being with others in a "subject-community" is not supported by his phenomenological ontology. Using the model he will later use in his *Critique* Sartre indicates the being of the worker as alienated insofar as he ostensibly experiences himself as an instrument for others whose work is not for his own sake but for others. Granting this model as relatively valid, we see that Sartre maintains that this conversion into an instrument is a submission to the projects of others. This is quite a different experience from my experience of "undifferentiated-being" when I am alone exercising an abstract transcendence. In passing into the social world, the world of community, I become, according to Sartre, anonymous, one amongst many anonymous others. Such a sense of being "lost in the they" (as Heidegger expressed it) is described by Sartre as a purely "psychological" experience and not an ontological condition. It is on this point that one must take issue with Sartre. How, one may ask, is this real experieence of a

---

25. *Ibid.,* p. 639.

real (actual or possible) state of being distinguishable from his previous descriptions? Can Sartre legitimately make this radical distinction between the psychological and the ontological in his own terms or in terms of his own notoriously psychologistic phenomenological ontology?

In his apparent zeal to avoid compromising his own phenomenology of being-for-others and the being of others for consciousness in the face of Heidegger's analyses of the realm of *das Man* (the anonymous world of impersonal social existence) and of *Mitsein,* Sartre separates his account of "the we-subject" from his previous ontology in a gratuitous way. First of all, it is quite clear that the description of my engagement in the "stream" of social life, in the "common rhythm" of daily existence is as much a part of my being and mode of existence as my being-for-others or my being determined as belonging to a group by a third person. What is called the "double objectivizing apprehension of the object transcended in common and of the bodies which surround mine"[26] is an intentional consciousness of something in my field of consciousness and is an "objectivizing" process in which I am engaged despite the contingent fact that the object (e.g., "the station 'La Motte-Picquet-Grenelle'") is presumably an object for a plurality of others. The characterization of this mode of being in a "subject-community" as a surrender of my transcendence to the transcendence of the "collective rhythm" (e.g., riding in a subway, waiting on a platform for the next train. etc.) is not significantly different from any concrete situation in which I find myself and is closely associated with my being in association with others in a work situation. Surely it is simply false to say that I merely "constitute myself as an undifferentiated transcendence" when pursuing ostensible "collective ends." For, one uses a subway or other "collective" objects in order to realize *personal* projects. Again, while apparently immersed in the world of the anonymous "they" I may be thinking about resolving a personal problem, about an intellectual puzzle, about my relations with a "significant other," etc., etc. My engagement with others in such circumstances may certainly be an authentic being with others as well as a passive surrender to the impersonal world of collective projects. Sartre's reason for not admitting the experience of "a we-subject" mode of being is simply indefensible in terms of his own phenomenological psychology. For, he unconvincingly argues that:

> ... whereas in the experience of being-for-others the upsurge of a dimension of real and concrete being is the condition for the very experience, the experience of the We-subject is a pure psychological, subjective event in a single consciousness; it corresponds to an inner modification of the

---

26. *Ibid.,* p. 497

structure of this consciousness but does not appear on the foundation of a concrete ontological relation with others and does not realize a *Mitsein*.[27]

That there is this distinction between Sartre's psychologistic account of being-for-others and this "way of feeling myself in the midst of others" is extremely questionable. All of his previous accounts of ontological relationships with others have had the same psychological, subjective form. Thus, for example, the *feeling* of alienation experienced when I sense that I am an object for the other is correlative to the feeling of alienation experienced in the midst of a crowd. If I act in a boisterous or outlandish manner in an elevator, I may suddenly feel shame when *le regard* of not one, but many, fixes me in an awkward situation. All in all, there is simply no justification for Sartre's attempt to treat the experience of "the we- subject" in isolation from his previous descriptions of our modes of being in relation to others. As if aware that he has stumbled upon something he is not (in *Being and Nothingness*) willing to deal with, he notes, *en passant*, that the sense of "we" "overcomes the original conflict of transcendences by making them converge in the direction of the world." This is precisely a point he should have seized upon since what he saw was the dominant factor of collective *cooperation* in a social context. What is astonishing in man's daily social life (e.g., in the subways in New York city during the rush hour) is the relatively few incidents of serious conflict which do occur even under the most intolerable conditions. But Sartre could not emphasize this too much considering his prior commitment to the notion that the primordial relation between man and man is characterized by conflict and tension.

If it is the case that my experience of the We-subject is of such a nature that it is viable only within certain organizations in the world (and vanishes with the disappearance of these organizations) this is *a fortiori* the case with my experience of "us-objects." Even if we grant to Sartre the view that the sense of a "subject-community" is not primary (presumably in an ontological sense), this does not mean it is not a significant dimension of my being. As I mentioned previously, Sartre's attempt to provide a phenomenology of the experience of the concrete existence of others is somewhat artificial and lacks a social field in which such an encounter ordinarily takes place. Only in the interior processes of thought could I encounter the other in the worldless, pure relationship of reciprocal negation. In actuality, as Sartre will later admit, I encounter the other in a social milieu, in a world already constituted by systems of meanings I have not created. The impersonal social relationships previously mentioned are

---

27. *Ibid.*

referred to by Sartre in a kind of grudging acknowledgement that, in fact, the waiter sees me as a customer, the ticket collector sees me as a patron, etc. In addition, he avers that "my professional and technical relations with others make me known to myself as anybody."[28] While it is true to some extent that such relationships are often impersonal, they are also a way in which I understand an aspect of myself and, moreover, they are clearly significant dimensions of my relations with others. As I have said earlier, it is not only others who define us in relation to our social roles, but we often define ourselves precisely in this way (partially, if not completely). This is not merely a subjective, psychological discovery; rather, it is a discovery of our being as social persons. In recognizing the social roles of others and the significations in the social world (e.g., the "Exit" sign in a building) even Sartre is led to admit that "I adapt myself to the human order . . . I recognize the Other's existence; I set up a dialogue with the Other."[29] If this is the case, why does Sartre hesitate to include these significant dimensions of human reality in his phenomenological ontology of the existence of, and the concrete encounter with, others? Is it simply because he wants to insist upon the priority of his ontology of others over that of Heidegger? This seems to be the case when he remarks that Heidegger did provide a useful analysis of *Mitsein* (or, for that matter, *(Mit-Dasein)* but he neglected to see that:

> . . . in order for the object to appear as manufactured, it is necessary that the Other be first given in some other way. A person who had not already experienced the Other would in no way be able to distinguish the manufactured object from the pure materiality of a thing which has not been worked on.[30]

In this regard, Sartre wants to insist that the recognition of instrumental objects as human creations presupposes a prior familiarity with others. Hence, he claims that the experience of a "we-subject" is a subordinate and derivative experience. This argument Sartre brings against Heidegger's notion of *Mitsein* cuts against some of his own basic notions. For, in the initial stages of his presentation of our experience of others he remarked that the identification of an "instrumental-thing" refers us immediately to "a plurality of for-itselfs." Indeed, it is sometimes suggested that our immediate apprehension is not of others in a world, but of in-

---

28. *Ibid.*, pp. 497-499.
29. *Ibid.*, p. 499: " . . . je m'accommode de l'ordre humain; je reconnais par mon acte même l'existence de l'autre, j'établis un dialogue avec l'autre."
30. *Ibid.*

strumental complexes (which, as we have seen, imply the existence of conscious others). That is:

> The consciousness of man in action is non-reflective consciousness. It is consciousness of something, and the transcendent which discloses itself to this consciousness is of a particular nature; it is a structure of exigency in the world, and the world correlatively discloses in it complex relations of instrumentality.[31]

Against Sartre, I would maintain that the experience of the "we- subject" is a significant aspect of our being-in-the-world in relation to others in a social milieu. The apprehension of such human relationships does not depend upon prior forms of the for-others, but is equiprimordial with the recognition of others who are already engaged in a world comprised of a multiplicity of significations, meanings, and instrumental objects. It is not the case that there is no symmetry between the experience of the "Us-object" and the experience of the "we-subject" insofar as both are clearly socially determined modes of human existence. Sartre's view that the latter form of relationship is merely "a psychological experience realized by an historic man immersed in a working universe and in a society of a definite economic type"[32] is a weak argument for the exclusion of the experience of a "subject-community" from his ontology. For, it is surely a significant fact that one dimension of human facticity is being-in-a- society comprised of a multiplicity of other human beings. To dismiss this awareness of being-with others as a mere "subjective *Erlebnis*" is to put in jeopardy most of his previous analyses, analyses which have often been described as dominated by a "subjective orientation." This subjective orientation has pervaded his descriptions of being-for-itself, being-in-itself and being-for-others. If it is true that "the for-itself is the being by which existents reveal their mode of being," then there is no reason why man's socio-historical existence should fall outside Sartre's general ontology. It is only by analyzing the immediate relations between man and man in abstraction from the actual social framework in which such relations occur that Sartre can declare that man's being-with others in society presupposes a more elementary encounter with others.

The "perpetual possiblility of *acting*" which is ascribed to consciousness refers to an actual modification of being-in-itself in its factual

---

31. *Ibid.*, p. 74.
32. *Ibid.*, p. 502. Cp. Sartre's earlier equation of each subjective consciousness with the *Erlebnis* which he later suggests cannot provide any ontological insight, Concrètement, chaque pour-soi (erlebnis) particulier . . . " [*EN*, p. 139]

(or ontic) materiality. What this means, in effect, is that the for-itself or consciousness acts through the body in a world comprised of things and others with whom any number of complex relationships are possible. These latter relationships must be social relationships in a world. Insofar as the emergence of the other occurs for consciousness, the other now "confers on the for-itself a being-in-itself-in-the-midst-of-the-world." This mode of being is the basis for what Sartre calls the coefficient of adversity which is purely human and which, in the final analysis, is the most important limiting factor in man's concrete freedom. For, it is chiefly the freedom of others which limits my concrete freedom in the world and which is an inescapable facticity. Whereas my free projects — in a purely theoretical sense — may be said to encounter resistance in things which emerges because of these projects, the inhibition of the realization of many of my projects is the existence of the conflicting projects of the insurpassable others. Our intentional concrete action is more often blocked by the human coefficient of adversity than by the coefficient of adversity in things. These are, it seems to me, some of the implications of Sartre's analysis of being-for-others.

In the concluding discussion of the concrete relations with others as well as in the description of the complex "circle" of relationships between individual consciousness and the other, Sartre had prepared the ground, as it were, for a social phenomenology. The implicit dialectical form of the relationships between man and man is made explicit in the *Critique*. In addition, the concept of the third man will reappear in his later social thought as a significant theme and the somewhat truncated account of the subject-community will be the starting point for his analysis of the social relations amongst men. Finally, the casual mention of historic man immersed in a working universe will become the search for the concrete universal — the individual historical man — in Sartre's later ambitious project. In point of fact, many of the minor themes in *Being and Nothingness* will eventually become major themes in his attempt to graft a social philosophy onto his individualistic existentialism. It is primarily the conception of being-for-others which locates man in a social world, a world in which freedom is truly circumscribed. In the interiority of consciousness I may be absolutely free; but in the social world in the presence of others there is an inherent limitation upon my freedom.

The analysis of being-for-others in *Being and Nothingness* is, for the most part, a rather abstract analysis, one which lacks a vital context. In this sense, it is quite correct to say that:

> . . . it is a partial work because the social world has a role in it only as an obstacle or barrier to the individual and his most fundamental aspirations. It is

not until the *Critique de la raison dialectique* that Sartre will examine mobile social reality with the same thoroughness.[33]

What I have suggested up to this point is that the rudiments of this later concern can be found in Sartre's earlier phenomenological ontology even in regard to terminological detail. The transition to a living dialectic of action is not an abrupt one, but a gradual change in perspective and emphasis. "Doing" or *faire* had already been described as one of the cardinal categories of human reality. What was needed was a social milieu in which human action could be effective as well as a technique by which to describe the complex network of human interactions. Sartre found this technique in the social dialectic.

---

33. Joseph H. McMahon, *Humans Being: The World of Jean-Paul Sartre*, Chicago and London, 1971, pp. 90-91.

III. THE SOCIAL DIALECTIC

> *"This dialectic process which consciousness executes on itself — on its knowledge as well as its object — in the sense that out of it the new and true object arises, is precisely what is termed experience."*
>
> G. W. F. Hegel,
> The Phenomenology of the
> Mind, "Introduction."

    The development of a conception of society as comprised of numerous processes of interaction, interrelationship, conflict, opposition and reciprocity in Sartre's social philosophy had been influenced, obviously, by the thought of Hegel, as well as by Marx's conception of social and historical change or movements. In the case of Hegel we see a consideration of an immanent spiritual dialectic not only in human history (conceived of in terms of the manifestation, through successive stages, of the Absolute in time), but in the "contradictions" in the world of actuality. There is, for Hegel, a dialectic in human experience as well as in thought itself. However, it would seem that all dialectical tendencies are ultimately subject to a kind of deductive necessity which seems to deprive individuals of any real freedom. Kierkegaard followed Hegel up to a point by declaring that "everything is dialectical." But he added a significant qualification by arguing that the various dialectical processes of reflection, spiritual development, psychological processes, etc., are contingent, not necessary. The "dialectic of life" is sustained by individuals by virtue of repeated choice and resoluteness. Primarily, it is the notion of a contingent dialectic sustained by the free *praxis* of individuals in a social milieu which itself is the realm of a social dialectic generated by a multiplicity of individual and group actions which concerns Sartre in his description of an experiential dialectic which he opposes to the dogmatic dialectic of nature which is defended by dogmatic Marxists. Generally speaking, Sartre's conception of a critical and experiential dialectic emerged out of the post-Marxian interpretations of socio-historical phenomena which developed in France in the post-war period.

The precise relationship between Sartre's conception of a social dialectic and Marx's notion of dialectic is a complex question because of the difficulty of determining what Marx's general understanding of dialectical processes was and because Sartre's use of Marx's sociological principles is eclectic. Although Marx described the internal changes in capitalism (at a particular stage of its development) in dialectical terms, it is not clear that he applied dialectical analyses to the infrastructure of social processes. The primary dialectical opposition for Marx was that between classes. *The Eighteenth Brumaire of Louis Napoleon Bonaparte* is, however, one of the few works in which Marx approached a concrete historical event by means of an interpretation that was strictly dialectical. In his later works — particularly *Das Kapital* — he tended to move from some dialectical analyses of capitalist society to an emphasis upon underlying *causal* factors in a kind of uni-directional notion of socio-historical causation. Sartre makes reference to Marx's study of the *Eighteenth Brumaire,* remarking that it is to be contrasted to contemporary, superficial Marxist analyses. It is said that Marx had attempted in this analysis "a difficult synthesis of intention and result." In addition, he makes reference to Marx's response to a review of *Das Kapital* which appeared in the *Courrier européen* to the effect that the reviewer seems to understand *his* method, but the question of *the* dialectical method remains open. This reference raises the question of the extensiveness of Marx's conception of dialectical relations in history and society. Of course, it is a debatable question whether Sartre is entirely justified in making a radical distinction between the dogmatism of present-day Marxists and the ostensibly nondogmatic approach of Marx himself.[1] This is, of course, a larger issue which is only tangentially related to my primary concern with the origin and nature of Sartre's social dialectic.

The development of a complex social dialectic in Sartre's social philosophy emerged out of a context in which a reasonably mature dialectical sociology had already been developed by Georges Gurvitch. To my

---

1. In a fine description of the development of Marxist thought, Z. A. Jordan has indicated the shift of emphasis of Marx's writings from sociological description to economic determinism (e.g. in *Das Kapital*) which is accompanied by an increasing dogmatism. [*The Evolution of Dialectical Materialism,* New York, 1967]. For a counter-argument to the effect that there is a continuity in Marx's thought in regard to his concern with social structures and social processes, one may refer to Henri Lefebvre's *The Sociology of Marx,* New York, 1968. In many respects Lefebvre's study seems to be directed against Sartre's *Critique* insofar as Lefebvre presents a sympathetic interpretation of Marx's social thought which touches upon many aspects of Sartre's later work (e.g., the meaning and role of *praxis,* the social dialectic, the development of social classes, etc.). That Sartre's

individualistic interpretation of the meaning of Marxism is not far from Lefebvre's mind is indicated in his criticism of Sartre's notion of the anthropology implicit in Marxism. Lefebvre remarks that Sartre, like Feuerbach, neglects practical-sensory activity as well as practical-critical or revolutionary activity (p. 33). In addition, he specifically charges that the concept of a "practico-inert" in inadequate to deal with real social *praxis*. In general, he criticizes him for adopting the "philosophical attitude" of Feuerbach's earlier anthropology. On each point of Lefebvre's casual criiticisms of Sartre I believe he is mistaken or is deliberately distorting Sartre's thought. Thus, for example, it is false that Sartre "overlooks the subjective aspect of sensory perception" or that he ignores "the activity that fashions the object, that recognizes it, and itself in it." At no point in his study of Marx's sociology does Lefebvre confront Sartre's interpretations head on nor does he even suggest the richness of his conception of a social dialectic. There is little doubt that Lefebvre considers Sartre a "liberal voluntarist" who has misunderstood Marx. Needless to say, there is no mention of the actual dogmatic sclerosis which has permeated recent Marxism — which of course, is precisely Sartre's target in his prefatory essay and the first part of the introduction of the *Critique* ("Dialectique Dogmatique et Dialectique Critique").

Raymond Aron believes that Sartre's social thought bears little relation to that of Marx. He remarks that "The dialectic of the series and the group, of the practico-inert and revolutionary praxis is obviously Sartrian, not Marxist. It supposes that individual action is the only dialectical and practical reality, the motive force behind everything." Aron points out that Sartre seems more interested in reconciling a philosophy of personal destiny with a philosophy of collective salvation than with the details of Marx's socioeconomic theories. *Vide: Marxism and the Existentialists,* New York, 1969, pp. 172-173.

In a recent study of Marx's thought, an anomalous opinion about the relation between Sartre and Marx is expressed. It is said that "Existentialism can . . . play the part of a corrective to present-day Soviet orthodoxy, by restoring the credit of a subjectivity long suppressed in the latter's objectivistically curtailed conception of dialectics . . . Sartre's mode of argument is not exclusively based on his existentialist doctrine, but just as much on positions which had been reached within the framework of Marxism itself long ago." Alfred Schmidt, *The Concept of Nature in Marx,* New York, 1972, p. 166.

In regard to Sartre's charge that Marxist thought (and the dialectic) has become dogmatic, it has been said that, in fact, it is Sartre's concept of dialectic that is truly dogmatic. In his "insistance plus forte sur le caractére essentiellement humain de la dialectique réele et les degrés multiples des médiations, Sartre se révelé incomparablement plus dogmatique que Marx, aussi bien dans sa conception générale de la dialectique que dans ses applications á la sociologie." *Dialectique et Sociologie,* p. 226.

Despite the numerous studies in recent years dealing with Sartre's "Marxism," there has still been no detailed analysis of the precise relationship between the *Critique* and the thought of Marx or the Marxist. Such an analysis would be quite difficult since it would require an understanding of Marx's use of, or conception of, dialectic, the development of dialectical theory in Marxist thought and a grasp of Sartre's notion of an immanent social dialectic. An interesting contribution to this general area of concern is Gurvitch's *Dialectique et Sociologie.*

Sartre's charges against a sclerotic, dogmatic Marxism are clearly inappropriate to the liberalization of Marxist thought in the works of Kolakowski or Adam Schaff. The latter's recent work, *Marxism and the Human Individual,* could be seen as lending partial support to Sartre's attempt to fuse existential individualism and Marxism.

mind, it is Gurvitch's sociology which is the primary influence on Sartre's approach to social phenomena. Many of the details of Gurvitch's sociology provide a clear introduction to the language and form of Sartre's understanding of society and the complex network of relationships which comprise it. Although Sartre does not follow Gurvitch's description of a social dialectic in every detail, the general orientation to social phenomena and social processes in Sartre's *Critique* is obviously indebted to Gurvitch's schema of the form of social relations and group dynamics.

Dialectical Hyperempiricism

The specific reference that Sartre makes to the thought of Gurvitch occurs in a context in which he is concerned with a clarification of the proper method of socio-historical interpretation and description. In developing his own conceptions of dialectical experience and dialectical reason Sartre is concerned to avoid dogmatic Marxism while retaining some of the sociological principles of Marx.

Although Sartre admits that American sociology has made significant advances, he claims that it is based upon an unstable theoretical foundation. Identifying the objective approach of American sociology as a form of positivistic hyperempiricism, Sartre refers to its tendency to focus upon fixed totalities (material instruments, social groups and institutional organization) to the exclusion of dynamic processes of "totalization" — i.e., the activity by which individuals or groups organize parts or elements into developing dynamic wholes. In addition, it is charged that objective sociology endeavors to treat the observer as if he were external to "the experimental field." In regard to this question, Sartre argues that the only valid approach to knowledge of social processes is that derived from microphysics: the observer is involved in the operational process of observation or there is a dialectical relationship between the knower and the known. The corresponding notion in Gurvitch's sociology is the "principle of complementarity" which is also derived from the process of interaction between observer and observed in microphysics.

Sartre maintains that a synthesis of hyperempiricism and dialectical understanding of the interrelationship of the subjective and the objective, interiority and exteriority, and a sense of the historical factors contributing to the directionality of social processes could be considered as a *moment* or stage in "the movement of historical totalizations." Such a synthesis could produce a:

> . . . sociology which will maintain the relative irreducibility of social fields, which will bring out — at the heart of the general movement —

the resistances, the checks, the ambiguities, the uncertainties . . . the very development of the dialectical philosophy must lead it to produce in a single act — the horizontal synthesis and the totalization in depth.[2]

This proposed fusion of a form of hyperempiricism and a dialectic was suggested to Sartre both by the historical analyses of Georges Lefebvre's *La Revolution française* [Paris, 1930-1957] and the sociological theory of Georges Gurvitch. The former's approach to historical understanding emphasized that the apparently "independent factors" in a historical process tend to lead to an event which develops itself in accordance with the schema of totalizing individuals or groups. Sartre approves of Lefebvre's notion that "history is not one thing," that there is no monistic *a priori* appropriate to history and that history "obeys diverse laws." The orientation Lefebvre adopts towards historical processes is related, by Sartre, to Gurvitch's concept of a *hyperempirisme dialectique*. Gurvitch had argued that a conscientious use of the method of hyperempiricism would reveal a dialectical structure in the interrelationships among microsociological phenomena. Such a method includes the assumption that we should take the object as such which gives itself and develops itself freely before our eyes, "that social facts give themselves in experience as dialectical phenomena and that the reciprocity of perspectives in social existence are founded on past experiences and prove themselves in the course of present experience." In addition, a hyperempirical dialectic is open to the use of dialectical interpretations, of an analytical determinism or other types of rationality.[3] What seems to attract Sartre to this general orientation towards socio-historical phenomena is its pluralistic approach to the understanding of social and historical events, its refusal of a blanket monistic method of understanding.

In order to see more clearly what this method or orientation entails, we will turn to Gurvitch's original formulation of a hyperempirical dialectic in the context of a larger sociological theory. Gurvitch believed that by pushing empiricism and relativism to their limit he could discover and formulate a dialectical hyperempiricism which would serve as a means of disclosing the complex intersection of the web of social relations. Primarily, social phenomena would be understood in terms of a "dialectic of complementarity" which would include the observer as an element in sociological inquiry. Furthermore, he stressed the importance of recogniz-

---

2. *CRD*, p. 58.
3. *Ibid.*, p. 117. In Klaus Hartmann's *Sartres Sozialphilosophie*, [Berlin, 1966, p. 57] it is erroneously reported that Sartre's sole reference to Gurvitch is on page 130 of the *Critique*.

ing mutual implication, ambivalence, polarity and the reciprocity of perspectives in social reality. Microsociology, or the study of "social electrons," would, he thought, uncover the basic types of groupings, social classes and global societies. As is the case in Sartre's *Critique*, the proper movement of sociological inquiry is from microsociological phenomena to macrosociological phenomena, from the individual social agent to global societies which penetrate history. Gurvitch's hyperempirical study of social relations disclosed structural and astructural social tendencies, highly organized social "totalities," as well as diffuse (or *de fait* social assemblies — corresponding to what Sartre calls serialities). The dynamic nature of social reality would be approached from the standpoint of sociology, history and ethnology. What a hyperempircism would make plain would be the complex interrelationship of horizontal social relations and vertical social relations. Gurvitch traces social relationships from the smallest social units to their manifestation in global societies playing a role in history. In this regard, Sartre follows Gurvitch in seeing no radical bifurcation between sociology and history.

Gurvitch argued that the study of dynamic social phenomena from a variety of perspectives would lead one to discover actual, immanent dialectical relationships in what he called "total social phenomena." In Gurvitch's case (as in Sartre's) it is held that a hyperempirical study of societies in movement would lead one to derive a dialectical method from the social processes themselves. That is, a dialectical sociology does not begin with the *a priori* assumption that social relations and processes are in themselves dialectical. Rather, it develops in relation to the nature of its subject-matter itself. As Sartre correctly points out, Gurvitch's dialecticism is itself empirically derived *(son dialecticisme est une condition elle-meme empirique)*.

The general orientation toward social phenomena adopted by Sartre in the *Critique* is Gurvitch's dialectical hyperempiricism understood as having a "provisional character." For Sartre, the only possibility that a dialectic exists is discovered in "the unity of a dialectical movement" itself. A social dialectic is originally discovered in "the living logic of action" and creates itself anew in each individual *praxis*. The dialectic is discovered as "the rationality of practice." Insofar as the dialectic is a totalizing activity of individuals or groups it is empirically rooted in "lived" social relations amongst men. For Sartre, the dialectic (if, as he reiterates, it exists) is not the *result* of social processes or of history. Rather, it is intelligible in lived social experience, in the original movements of totalization and in the totalization *en cours* which comprises the dynamics of social existence. Man is capable of understanding the social dialectic because his experience itself is dialectical. Rather than demonstrating that this is the case, Sartre tries to show the dialectical nature of individual and group actions in his social phenomenology. In this regard, he is not so much concerned with reiterating the claim of Gurvitch to derive a dialectical conception of society from a hyperempirical study of social processes, but to determine the conditions that would have to be assumed in order to justify the acceptance of a method of dialectical empiricism. What must be borne in mind is that Sartre's general approach to a social phenomenology is provisional and hypothetical in form, despite the fact that it is clear that he believes that only a hyperempirical dialectic is viable for an in-depth understanding of complex social relationships. Despite the provisos of merely hypothetical consideration, and despite Sartre's emphases upon what has been disclosed at various "stages" in the development of his social philosophy (which itself seems to be designed to illustrate the dialectical development of his thought), it is Gurvitch's dialectical hyperempiricism which is the basic model for Sartre's account of social reality.

Social Determinism and Freedom

If Gurvitch's conception of a dialectical hyperempiricism is the kind of methodological and descriptive instrument Sartre sees as most applicable to the social world, his understanding of the nature of social determinism is also, to some extent, indebted to Gurvitch's dialectical sociology. One of the central themes of the *Critique* is the dialectical tension between individual freedom and the deterministic structures which arise in a social milieu. Gurvitch, too, had been concerned with preserving the freedom of the individual in a world in which there are networks of deterministic relationships.

Specifically, Gurvitch had tried to show — in *Les déterminismes sociaux et liberté humaine* — how individual freedom and social determinism interact. He argued that there are pathways of freedom which cut through, or emerge within, different social frameworks. The individual's "innovative freedom" is preserved in Gurvitch's account insofar as it is held that "partial determinisms" arise in a social matrix which are not elements or factors in an encompassing deterministic system. The notion of partial determinisms (which Sartre adopts in his sociological description) entails the denial that social determinism (unlike the universal determinism assumed to hold for all macrophysical phenomena in nature) is uniform, universal or pervasive. Rather, it may be said to emerge in certain social situations and then dissipate, become a diffuse system of relationships which provides for pathways of freedom. As Gurvitch expresses it, "the plurality of social determinisms . . . are always partial" and characterized by "relative unification." There are "scales of determinism" which are manifested in large-scale social unities.[4] In the interstitial zones which are open by virtue of the partial nature of the plurality of social determinisms the individual is able to express his freedom in spontaneous action. It is such individual freedom which is the origin of the unpredictable and the unexpected. The conception of the intrasocial freedom of the individual in Gurvitch's thought creates a tension between the individual and the interpersonal, collective groups in society. That is, there is a dialectical interpenetration of the individual, others (individuals or groups) and the totality of society itself. In this regard, Gurvitch insists that:

> Neither the individual nor society is able to exist without the other . . . The individual is immanent in society and society is immanent in the individual. From this reciprocal immanence one finds society anew in the depth of the 'Me' and discovers once again the 'Me' in the depth of the 'We.'[5]

In describing the tendencies towards structure and toward astructural phenomena, Gurvitch retains a conception of the uncertainty, the stochastic processes which seem to emerge in the interaction of social forces. This is not to say that dialectical hyperempiricism subscribes to a form of indeterminism. Rather, it places emphasis upon the interpenetration of various strata of social reality and upon the tenuous, paradoxical and dialectical relationships discoverable in society. These conceptions, in coordination with a notion of the dialectical relationship among elements in society and the dynamic totality of society *en acte* (or Sartre's process of totalization), led Gurvitch to say that within a "social *Gestalt*" there is a dynamic interplay of individual freedom and partial, temporary and contingent determinism. The "inventive liberty" of individuals is always in a relation of tension to the social determinisms which have a temporary, but objective, existence. All social entities are conceived of as in a "precarious equilibrium" which is comprised of multiple hierarchies. What Gurvitch discerns in his depth sociology is both partial determinisms *and* concrete contingencies which allow for the possibility of the unexpected and the unplanned. There is continuity in social processes and discontinuity. Social change is brought about both from the interior perspective of the individual or the group and by the momentum of exterior social or material forces. Finally, social reality is characterized by tendencies towards struc-

---

4. Georges Gurvitch, *Mon itineraire intellectuelle*, Paris, 1958, p. 18. Cited in P. Bosserman, *Dialectical Sociology*, Boston, 1968, p. 53.
5. Georges Gurvitch, *La vocation actuelle de la sociologie*, Paris, 1950, I, p. 37.

tural unification and "destructuralization," consolidation and polarization, unifying and conflicting "reciprocities of perspective."

The outcome of Gurvitch's existential sociology is that hyperempiricism as a method of interpreting social phenomena discloses a complex network of dialectical relations within a society conceived of as a "totality *en marche.*" In this regard, Gurvitch (and Sartre as well) notes the striking affinity between the dialectic as a method, as a real movement, and experience. The ultimate foundation for this immanent dialectic is the "human factor" or man's lived-experience as a dynamic process which expresses in action the "sinuosities, complexities, flexibilities and tensions" of social existence. Although he does not refer to the distinction, there is implicit in his sociological analysis the distinction Sartre makes between the dialectic of individual *praxis* and the dialectic generated by the totalizing activities of other individuals or groups. These processes are not, of course, isolated one from the other; rather, they interact in the totality in process which is society. What is absent from Gurvitch's thought (though present in Sartre's sociology) is any attempt to formulate a conception of dialectical reason. We will turn to a consideration of Sartre's concept of dialectical reason after further consideration of the background of Sartre's social dialectic.

Sartre maintains that the dialectic is both a method and a movement immanent in its "objects." In regard to human history alone it has a higher degree of heuristic value despite its questionable application to natural processes. The specific problem that Sartre is concerned with in developing a provisional conception of a social dialectic (modeled, to some extent, on Gurvitch's dialectical hyperempiricism) is, "under what conditions is a dialectic able to be founded?" The answer he gives to his question is that the foundation of dialectic is the critical experiences of social agents. Although the socio-historical dialectic is initiated and sustained by individual *praxis,* the individual submits to the dialectic (in social action) insofar as he makes it and he makes it insofar as he submits to it.[6] A dialectic discloses itself only to an observer situated in the interior of a social field. In this regard, as we have said, the observer does not have a privileged vantage-point in relation to the social phenomena he studies. If there is a social dialectic, it does not reveal itself to "contemplative reason." Rather, it can only be discovered "in the course of *praxis*".

The critical (or self-conscious, intentional) experience of the individual engaged in social action is itself "a real moment in the totalization *en cours*" which is itself a manifestation of the dialectic in the world. It is

---

6. *CRD*, p. 131.

the lived-experience of individuals which initiates "the dynamic relations of different social structures." Aside from the impingement of the past — through already constituted institutions, groups, instrumental complexes and social practices — on the critical experience of social agents (as dialectically conditioned), action in a social milieu involves an encounter with social determinisms presently operative. The dialectic of *praxis* brings about the appearance of novelty in the social world, as well as the reorganization of the "practical field." Purposeful, creative action unifies the "molecular dispersion" of utensils or social multiplicity. In doing so, however, the individual finds himself in a network of social relations (or in a socio-material matrix) which limits his freedom. That is, he acts in a realm in which there is a "dialectical circularity." Such a circularity is shown by the way in which individual experience is the foundation of an assembly and the assembly produces the individual in his reality as a social agent.[7] Because the subjective individual acts within practical fields that are already constituted (i.e., conditioned by the past, by inert material or social factors, by other individuals or groups), he discovers apparently impersonal social forces (e.g., "actions without agents, productions without producers, counterfinalities," etc.) which circumscribe his freedom. Social action involves the attempt to surpass the limitations of a situation through the process of realizing projects. However, even though man as a productive social agent determines the regions, systems and objects in an "inert totality," he encounters *determinations partielles* ("partial determinations") in the unified environment.[8]

Since work is the permanent form in which dialectical experience is expressed (or 'lived'), man is necessarily subject to the partial determinations of the material universe, as well as to the determinations of inertial social entities. Individual *praxis* is inseparable from the practical milieu it constitutes and which, in turn, constitutes it. Man exists for man only in the given social conditions and circumstances which are themselves the dialectical consequence of the activity of men. The partial determinisms which Sartre introduces into his social phenomenology are either generated by the rebounding of individual *praxis* upon itself or by the totalizing activity of others or, finally, by the original dependent relation man has to "materiality." The relation between the subjective individual and these partial determinations is itself dialectical. Sartre agrees with Gurvitch in holding that the "creative freedom" of the individual is expressed in "a determined social field" which is not a rigid system of causal

---

7. *Ibid.*, p. 155.
8. *Ibid.*, p. 173.

relations, but is comprised of partial, contingent and temporal determinations. The repeated emphasis in the *Critique* on the diachronic (i.e., pertaining to change or development over a period of time, as in natural languages) aspects of social phenomena is directly related to Gurvitch's conception of the various types of social time and their effects upon social units.[9] The discontinuity of social time is clearly related to the durational character of emergent and contingent social determinations, and is a notion which is implicit in Sartre's description of the various stages of the dialectic and of social formations. Although Sartre does not discuss what he means by the diachronic character of the partial determinisms which emerge in the social dialectic, his use of these notions seems compatible with Gurvitch's view that the conception of determinism cannot be detached from the concrete and real frameworks to which it pertains, that determinism is limited by the time in which it is viable and that social determinations are limited, relative and partial.[10] Although Sartre does not follow Gurvitch's sociological theory in every respect, there are a number of significant parallels which justify our placing Sartre's social phenomenology in the stream of dialectical sociology. In this regard, Sartre's sociological analyses are neither entirely original nor idiosyncratic.

Before turning to a consideration of Sartre's notion of dialectical reason, I will attempt to trace some of the threads of continuity from *Being and Nothingness* to the *Critique* (especially in regard to the situation of human freedom in a social world) and indicate residual analogies between the social thought of Gurvitch and that of Sartre.

Aside from the various discernible relationships between Gurvitch's dialectical sociology and Sartre's social phenomenology, we can also see certain lines of continuity from the phenomenological ontology to the later social phenomenology.[11] Thus, for example, Sartre had formulated a conception of the deterministic structure of the world in *Being and Nothingness* which viewed the natural world as a system of causal relationships which is alien to human freedom, but which had meaning only in reference to the intentionality of consciousness. Sartre had held that subjective consciousness, in situation, finds itself "engaged in being," "threatened by being," or face to face with the independence of things in

---

9. Georges Gurvitch, *The Spectrum of Social Time*, trans., M. Korenbaum and P. Bosserman, Dordrecht, Holland, 1964, pp. 26-33.
10. Georges Gurvitch, *Déterminismes sociaux et liberté humaine,* Paris, 1955, pp. 39-40.
11. The dialectical character of human relations in *Being and Nothingness* was pointed out by Gilbert Varet in his *L'Ontologie de Sartre* [Paris, 1948, p. 173] and has been suggested as a point of departure for a social dialectic by K. Hartmann in *Sartres Sozialphilosophie* [Berlin, 1966, p. 26ff].

the world. The self-conscious individual is in a different mode of relationship to others insofar as they are discovered as conscious beings whose projects may be in conflict with my own. Man's existence in the world in relation to others is characterized by an encounter with a purely human coefficient of adversity (a notion retained and heightened by Sartre in the *Critique*). It is clear that the relationship between oneself and others, as described in *Being and Nothingness*, is one of the bases for a dialectical understanding of relationships amongst individuals in society. The phenomenological descriptions of the relations amongst individuals, concrete relations with others and concrete freedom in situation touched upon man's existence in a world of others and used terms which reappear in the *Critique*.

The questions raised in *Being and Nothingness* concerning concrete human action seemed to cry out for an expansion into a social world. Thus, when Sartre claims that:

> To act is to modify the *shape* of the world . . . to arrange means in view of an end . . . to produce an organized instrumental complex such that by a series of concatenations and connections the modification effected on one of the links causes modifications throughout the whole series and finally produces an anticipated result,[12]

we seem to lack the social framework in which such action could take place. A significant limiting factor in concrete action is relationship to the social reality of others. The question that remained was, what structure does this relationship have? In addition, we would want to know if social determinism is analogous to the universal determinism affecting things. Both of these questions were central to the concerns of Gurvitch in *Déterminismes sociaux et liberté humaine* and to those of Sartre in the *Critique*.

For both Gurvitch and Sartre, human freedom expresses itself concretely in a matrix of reciprocal relationships amongst individual and individual, "the other" and "We," and the dominant social classes. Gurvitch had said that the most elementary form of social rapport concerns the relations of "I," the "alter ego" (or other) and "We." The multidimensional social phenomena described in a dialectical sociology are initially based upon this fundamental interrelationship, an interrelationship expressed in actual societies in terms of "polarity," "ambiguity," "complementarity" and a "reciprocity of perspectives." Using language that Sartre will adopt almost *in toto*, Gurvitch describes a social whole or "totality" as:

> . . . a mobile . . . concrete system of equilibria based on a fusion of "reciprocal perspectives," a system which is dynamic and where the ir-

---

12. *L'Être et le néant*, p. 508

reducible elements of multiplicity and unity, individual and universal, tend to be synthesized in a fashion which is perpetually changing.[13]

Although Gurvitch accepts the ideal of the possibility of coordination, integration and cooperation with less reluctance than Sartre, he also realized that the dialectical interplay of the projects of individuals and others, groups and countergroups is often characterized by reciprocal antagonism. Sartre, like Gurvitch, seems to adopt what sociologists call a conflict paradigm of social relations. Given Sartre's rather pessimistic conception of human relationships (in *Being and Nothingness* as well as the *Critique*), it is not surprising that he emphasizes the conflicting nature of all forms of social relationship.

As we have seen, Sartre agrees with Gurvitch that the primary methodological access to complex social phenomena is neither the objectivism of Emile Durkheim (for whom social facts are *things*) nor the analytic structuralism of American sociology (especially, Talcott Parsons). Rather, a conception of "the rhythm of social reality" that will encompass structural and astructural social forms, microsociology and macrosociology, loosely structured groups as well as defined social classes is more comprehensive and inclusive than other orientations. The separation of the individual and the collectivity is a false notion which ignores the mutual interdependence of the individual and society. The dialectical relations between individual and others (foreshadowed in *Being and Nothingness*) is "immanent" in actual social frameworks.

As if attacking the early existentialism of Sartre, Gurvitch criticizes the concept of the "pure I" existing in complete autonomy, apart from all social relations. The individual is truly individual; but he becomes an individual in a social milieu which necessarily affects his personal existence. An individual conceived of as absolutely independent of others is an abstract self without any real existence. In this regard, Gurvitch maintains that "...social patterns guide and direct not only behavior, but also mental life itself, whether it be collective or individual."[14] In the *Critique*,

---

13. Georges Gurvitch, *L'idée du droit social*, Paris, 1932, p. 17. In his later work, *Dialectique et Sociologie*, Gurvitch specifically relates his conception of totalities to that of Sartre and approves of his notion that the dialectic is expressed in human existence. He asserts that *C'est à bon droit qu'il lie la dialectique à la condition humaine, à la praxis . . . se manifestant dans la vie des hommes, des groupes, des classes sociales, finalement dans la réalité historique, car tout mouvement dialectique porte les signes dans efforts humains. Sartre insiste . . . sur le fait que les totalités . . . dans la dialectique ne sont jamais des totalités toutes faites, statiques, mais des totalites en train de se faire ou de se refaire, totalités dynamiques, totalités mouvantes, totalities en marche, selon notre propre terminologie.*" [p. 204].
14. Georges Gurvitch, *La vocation actuelle de la sociologie*, Paris, 1950, I, pp. 73-74.

Sartre clearly abandons the perspective of abstract consciousness and conceives of the self in terms of its concrete action "in situation" or in the practical world of social relations. One could say that Sartre shifts his perspective from a consideration of the world for consciousness to consciousness "existing" the body in *praxis*. In a reference to *Being and Nothingness* he remarks that "the for-itself" is an agent which discovers itself, at first, as "inert . . . in the milieu of the in-itself." It is said that *praxis* "is always consciousness of self," a "non-thetic consciousness" which is nothing other than the practical affirmation that I am.[15] In this context Sartre makes a revealing, but ambiguous, remark which suggests an important change in Sartre's ontology. It is contended that the complex relation of the non-thetic consciousness affirmed in practice (and escaping oneself insofar as it constitutes oneself as other) to the practical world is what permits one to understand "why man *projects himself* . . . in the milieu of the in-itself-for-itself."[16] What this seems to suggest is that Sartre no longer thinks of "the in-itself-for-itself" as an impossible God, but as society or history.

In contrast to the general Marxian view that social roles express class membership, Gurvitch refers to the interpenetration of such roles and their contribution to processes of "structuration" and "destructuration." Social roles are described as the springboards for possible individual or collective actions. These social dimensions of the individual are not considered as contingent, anonymous characteristics of persons, but as means by which an individual (or a group) expresses freedom in a social matrix. It is the social totality which determines the viability of the "web of social roles" and is a determining factor affecting the limits of concrete freedom. As is the case in Sartre's description of social processes, Gurvitch does not create a radical separation of sociology proper and social psychology insofar as the domain of total social phenomena overlaps the psychological motivations of individual and groups. In this regard, social roles or functions are given a significant place in Sartre's psychologistic phenomenology of the social relations amongst men which is quite different from his disparagement of such roles in *Being and Nothingness*. In the *Critique*, Sartre seems to agree implicitly with Gurvitch's general view that human action is primarily expressed through a variety of social roles. The significant difference between Sartre and Gurvitch is that the former does not accept the latter's notion that there is a "collective psyche"[17] which is presumably

---

15. *CRD*, p. 286, n. 1.
16. *Ibid*.
17. Georges Gurvitch, *The Spectrum of Social Time*, p. 5. This notion of a collective psyche is criticized by Sartre in the form in which it was originally presented by Durkheim.

something over and above individual psychic states. In other respects, however, Sartre does seem to accept Gurvitch's emphases upon the overlapping of sociology and social psychology, the variability of social roles in a meaningful social framework and the actual determinations encountered in individual social action. More importantly, as we have seen, he adopts Gurvitch's central conception of the immanent dialectic in social processes.

The individual's relationship to groups in a social field covers a range of possible affiliations which extends from a "partial fusion" of individuals with others to societal communion (an ideal form of social integration in which conflict is minimized). Such social bonds are based upon elementary social relationships which contribute either to the creation of social structures or their disintegration. A basic partial determination of the individual is manifested in passive *de fait* groupings (corresponding to Sartre's concept of serialities) which affect the social existence of the individual. Sartre illustrates this kind of passive determination by referring to someone listening to the radio and being subject to a political broadcast. Such an individual experiences his "otherness" as one of many, as subject to an impotent receptivity. One is passively a part of a homogeneous collective milieu.[18] In addition to such diffuse social groupings there are imposed groupings (groups constituted by other groups) and voluntary associations. The relations of individuals within more organized groups are, for Gurvitch and Sartre, dialectical. Much of the material on group formations in Gurvitch's analysis of macrosociological features of social reality will find its way into Sartre's phenomenology of groups.

Clearly, the concept in Gurvitch's social thought that was most influential on Sartre's theory of social existence was that of partial determinism. There is no doubt that Gurvitch's notion of determinism suggested to Sartre a way to avoid the rather rigid conception of determinism which he had adhered to in *Being and Nothingness*. A notion of partial determinism would allow for the dialectical interaction of subjectivity and objectivity, for the innovative project which is "the subjective surpassing of objectivity" towards a new objectivity which Sartre desired to preserve. Gurvitch's description of determinism is, to my mind, the key to an understanding of Sartre's conception of the situation of man in the social world. Gurvitch avers that:

> Determinism is the integration of particular facts into one of the real, multiple frameworks or concrete universes (actual, known or constructed) which always remains contingent; it . . . situates these facts,

---

18. *CRD*, pp. 320-327.

that is explains them in relationship to its understanding of the framework. This integration presupposes, in effect, an understanding of the relative cohesion of the contingent framework in question, plus its unfolding life within one or several of the [social] temporalities.[19] This general conception of the relative cohesion of a social framework which is itself contingent and diachronic provided for a limited, temporary determinism which would not negate human freedom, but which stipulates the limitation of that freedom in particular social situations. As a social agent, man is determining in his *praxis* and is determined (or constituted) by others — insofar as their projects impinge upon one's own —, by groups, by inert material or social entities or by the rebound of one's own actions. In social action the individual *must* objectify himself and hence subject himself to the partial determinations which emerge in what Sartre describes as the "exteriority" of socio-material existence. While this general conception of determinism seems to be indirectly appealed to by Sartre in his account of the "dialectic of *praxis*" and his description of group-formations, his analysis of the role and place of the individual in organized groups leads him to refer to a *necessity* which is not justified by Gurvitch's conception of being in society. Sartre refers to the practical experience of necessity as a stage in the dialectic of social action. Necessity emerges in experience when *alteration* transforms individual action into action for others or when matter worked upon robs man of his action. The correlative form of the experience of necessity is *objectification* by virtue of the exterior "materialization" of *praxis*.[20] In the organized group, too, the individual is described as subject to (or, more accurately, subjecting himself to) the action of the group on its members. In Sartre's terms, one could say that this submission to necessity within groups involves alteration (in the sense that the individual becomes other for the others in the group) and objectification (insofar as the individual is objectified in the group in terms of his role and function).[21] Despite Sartre's reassurance that necessity is only a moment or stage in the dialectic of action or of group formation, and despite the fact that he says this necessity is not to be understood as "constraint," there is a real sense in which Sartre does admit a necessity in certain social processes and thereby surpasses Gurvitch's conception of the partial, temporary limitations of man's freedom in society. It is in his conception of the conversion of the individual into a "common-individual" (in coercive, pledged or organized groups) that Sartre comes closest to be-

---

19. Georges Gurvitch, *Déterminismes sociaux et liberté humaine*, p. 40.
20. *CRD*, pp. 279-285.
21. *Ibid.*, pp. 633-634.

traying the individual's freedom in society which he desires to preserve. Although there are variations on Gurvitch's themes in the *Critique*, they do not diverge too often from the central orientation in the former's sociology. Gurvitch's conception of the upsurge of the unexpected or the novel in social action, for example, is very much in evidence in Sartre's account of the role of individual and group *praxis*. In his *La vocation actuelle de la sociologie* Gurvitch creates a portrait of the dynamic eruption of "creative liberty" which has its analogue in Sartre's description of a creative social dialectic. Especially in Sartre's description of the storming of the Bastille do we find a concrete illustration of Gurvitch's overview of society in action. Synthesizing many of his basic notions, Gurvitch maintains that:

> One finds in the total social phenomena as they are expressed in the macrosociological frameworks . . . factors which lead to radical change: it is the constant testing by fire of . . . the "diffused milieux". . . they are the fugitive instants of social life, where groups, societies, humanity realize a consciousness of themselves . . . outside of the expected, the predictable, the anticipated . . . it is the . . . unexpected element, the . . . unforeseen, discontinuous, whole and concrete, and inseparable from a totality *en marche*. This totality is where . . . the *acte*, inventive liberty, decision-making liberty, and creative liberty cause an eruption in the social life beyond all that is foreseen. Such phenomena . . . subsist in the total social phenomena, be it global or partial, macrosociological or microsociological . . . In this respect, every structure . . . is a tributary of the total social phenomena as such, which it transcends while always at its base is this volcanic phenomenon which can never be fully expressed by the structure above.[22]

Sartre, like Gurvitch, tends to proceed, in his phenomenology of social relations, from the microsociological to the macrosociological and to conceive of society as such as a "totality *en marche*.". The originator of creative liberty is the individual who acts within a social world which is constituted by individual action as well as constituting (through partial determinations) such action. What is implicit in Gurvitch's description of individual social action is made explicit in Sartre's conception of man in the *Critique*. For, the individual is seen as the locus of intentional, originative action and as a mediator of social and material forces that act upon him and circumscribe his freedom of action. As I shall try to show, in the process of development from individual action to group organization there is a gradual loss of individual liberty and an increase in the coercive power of non-individual social forces. In his explication of the process of

---

22. Georges Gurvitch, *La vocation actuelle de la sociologie*, I, pp. 438-439.

dialectical movement, Sartre avers that it is the law of totalization *(la loi de totalisation)* which creates collectivities, societies and a history. These realities impose themselves on individuals; but, at the same time, they are "woven by millions of individual acts."[23] Without specifically referring to Gurvitch's understanding of the dialectic of social experience, Sartre describes the processes of social action and reaction, individual liberty and the determinate objective factors impinging on that liberty in the language of Gurvitch's sociology.

Although Sartre does not rigidly follow in Gurvitch's footsteps, the terminology he uses in the *Critique* and many of his central themes are clearly derived from the theoretical analysis of "depth levels" of social reality in Gurvitch's social thought. Sartre seems to adopt the following of Gurvitch's notions: (1) the dialectical nature of social experience, individual and group interactions; (2) the concept of the "reciprocity of perspectives;" (3) the close relationship between sociology and history; (4) the attempt to understand the life-history of social groups from the standpoint of their being;[24] (5) the spontaneity of individual social action; (6) the apprehension of total social phenomena within a sociohistorical framework; (7) the interpenetration of vertical and horizontal dimensions of social reality; (8) the complementarity of social observer and observed phenomena; (9) the inadequacy of the static theories of American "abstract empiricist" sociologists; (10) the concept of society as *en acte;* (11) the interaction of freedom and determinism in social processes; (12) the temporal structure of social actions or events; and (13) the general method of a dialectical hyperempiricism. In general, Sartre's approach to social phenomena echoes Gurvitch's stress upon the multidimensional rather than the unidimensional schema of social processes. This orientation towards social phenomena combined with what sociologists describe as a conflict paradigm of sociological interpretation is characterized by Gurvitch as an "existential sociology."

For both Gurvitch and Sartre, it is the "human factor" or the existential condition of man which is the basis of dialectical processes in society and not an impersonal metaphysical force immanent in nature. Man is able to understand dialectical processes in society because his experience is itself dialectical. Complementing the general conception of dialectical reason in Sartre's social phenomenology is a notion which has its analogy in Gurvitch's sociology. That is, the mode of knowledge of dialectical phenomena which is a form of *compréhension*. In the thought of Gurvitch

---

23. *CRD*, p. 131.
24. Cf. P. Bosserman, *Dialectical Sociology*, p. 283.

and Sartre the understanding of social phenomena is similar to the notion of *Verstehen* as employed by Dilthey and Weber. Gurvitch maintains that *compréhension* is not radically distinct from explanation insofar as explanation requires a general understanding of a total situation. In a remark that seems to lie at the basis of Sartre's idea of *compréhension* Gurvitch maintains that:

... it is as impossible to explain without understanding, as it is to comprehend the relative coherence of this latter without reaching some conclusion as to the manner of integration that is explanation.[25]

Sartre assumes that it is always theoretically possible to comprehend human conduct or human projects. An explanation of social action or social processes requires a form of comprehending "lived" determinations which are revealed in *praxis* and which are the basis for an "indirect" knowledge of the existence of others. That is, we explain our own social action in terms of an understanding of our personal projects and we explain the social actions of others by an indirect *compréhension* of the projects of others. Man is capable of a fundamental comprehension of the human reality in each individual. Such a form of comprehension is given in all *praxis*.[26]

Sartre is in agreement with Dilthey's general notion that the cultural order is not reducible to the natural order and that comprehension *(Verstehen)* is the means by which we "grasp the meaning of any human conduct." *Compréhension* is described as a "dialectical movement" which explains a social act by means of its terminal signification in reference to its initial condition. One understands the conduct of others in terms of a grasp of a synthetic situation in which the meanings of particular actions are clarified in reference to an understanding of the complete situation. We understand the "practical field" in which an action takes place and, hence, can explain the significance of particular acts. Comprehension requires a progressive grasp of the objective result intended and a regressive grasp of the "original condition" from which an action emerged. Intentional action unifies a practical field and reveals ("illuminates") the meaning of a concrete or material situation. For Sartre, as for Gurvitch, *compréhension* and explanation are inseparable. Understanding is "the totalizing movement which gathers together my neighbor, myself, and the environment in the synthetic unity of an objectification in process."[27] Insofar

---
25. Georges Gurvitch, *Déterminismes sociaux et liberté humaine*, p. 40.
26. *CRD*, pp. 105-106.
27. *Ibid.*, p. 97.

as individual or collective *praxis* is characterized by totalizing or synthesizing "movements," Sartre incorporates the notion of *compréhension* into his description of the dialectic of individual or collective action without referring to it explicitly. Although Sartre's conception of *compréhension* is not precisely identical to Dilthey's notion of *Verstehen* (conceived as a process of sympathetic reliving and reconstructing of the motives, purposes or intentions of social or historical agents on the basis of an analysis of objectivications or "expressions of life"), it is a variation on Dilthey's central theme. In this regard, Sartre's conception of the meaningful significations discovered in the world (and pointing back to a signifying agent) is analogous to Dilthey's concept of "objectifications of spirit." It should be mentioned that Sartre's conception of man as a signifying being or a "creator of signs" in the *Critique* is not a departure from earlier descriptions of man in *Being and Nothingness*. The point, at any rate, is that the notion of *compréhension* introduced in the *Critique* has its analogue in a similar conception in Gurvitch's sociology. Certainly, both Gurvitch and Sartre agree in integrating the sociological concept of *Verstehen* with a dialectical account of social processes.

Partially under the influence of Gurvitch and partially due to his recognition of the brute actuality of material or human "coefficients of adversity," Sartre has come to stress the limiting factors that inhibit, rebound upon, or restrain human freedom. That the sense of the restrictions on human freedom is not something which appears abruptly in Sartre's later thought is clear from his description of freedom in his essay "Materialism and Revolution." For, he had remarked that freedom is only discovered in action, that it is inseparable from action and forms the foundation of the interrelations which constitute the internal structure of such action. In what amounts to an anticipation of the problem he will deal with in his transcendental analysis of dialectical reason (i.e., the attempt to determine the conditions of its possibility and its limits), Sartre argues that:

> A revolutionary philosophy ought to account for the plurality of freedoms and show how each one can be an object for the other while being, at the same time, a freedom for itself. Only this double character of freedom and objectivity can explain the complex notions of oppression, conflict, failure and violence.[28]

It is clear that the complex interaction of subjective freedom and objectivity is the central theme of the *Critique*. Man is "located in the

---

28. J. P. Sartre, "Materialism and Revolution," in *Sartre: Literary and Philosophical Essays*, ed. A. Michelson, New York, 1962, pp. 243-251.

world," subject to a monistic, pervasive socio-historical dialectic which is characterized by a variety of stages and 'oppositions" which are moments in an immanent process originating in the concrete lived-experience of individuals. Men work within practical fields which condition their activities and which can be reworked, transformed and surpassed by innovative action. Human work itself — by which man creates and recreates his life — is entirely dialectical. One of the poles of this dialectical relationship is matter itself (the *en-soi* described in more determinate form) as well as the negation of dialectic through exteriority and plurality. That is, what Sartre calls the "practico-inert" field which is described as an "antidialectic" force which human *praxis* endeavors to surpass. As in the description of man's condition in concrete situation in *Being and Nothingness,* man is situated in the *Critique* in a world of practical instruments, significations, inert matter, in a realm of facticity which is independent of man. Although inert material beings are not, strictly speaking, absolutely independent of man as a consciousness-body, it is clear that both matter and others are considered not merely in referential relationship to consciousness, but as actual, independent entities which limit individual freedom. It is, in point of fact, these dual factors which are the primary sources of alienation. As Sartre expresses it:

> It is in the concrete and synthetic relation of the agent to the other through the mediation of the thing, and to the thing through the mediation of the other, that we find the basis of all possible alienation.[29]

Sartre has not, by any means, abandoned his fundamental belief that "man makes himself." He has, however, come to admit the actual power of causal and "antidialectical" factors which shape the already constituted world in which each man finds himself. The projection of the self into the socio-historical arena implies a limitation upon the concrete freedom of man, the only freedom which is now of interest to Sartre. He has taken Marx's assertion that "man makes his own history in circumstances he has not created" seriously. And he has, perhaps unintentionally, absorbed Heidegger's description of man's being-in-the world in its immediate form. That is, the dimension of practical involvement in a system of significations and tools which is dominated by a practical orientation of "circumspective concern." In many respects, the initial description of man as a signifying being owes as much to Heidegger's existential phenomenology as it does to Dilthey's conception of objectifications of life. For, in the *Criti-*

---

29. *CRD*, p. 154n.

que, man finds himself in a world which is already constituted — practically, socially, institutionally and historically — by the prior *praxis* of men. This notion is similar to Heidegger's phenomenological description of the basic, ordinary mode of man's *in-der-Welt-Sein* in *Being and Time*. The constituting factors in the human world are (a) inert matter; (b) the field of the practico-inert which is described as a material and inorganic field created or sustained (intentionally or unintentionally) by the collective actions of men or specific groups; and, finally, (c) the various negativities — primarily scarcity — which condition action and the emergence of the practico-inert field. These factors had been recognized by Sartre in *Being and Nothingness* in terms of the resistances or obstacles comprising the human and non-human "coefficients of adversity." Clearly, Sartre has not abandoned his fundamental assumption that human freedom requires the existence of obstacles to be overcome or surpassed. Thus, in his earlier work, he had remarked that:

> It is by means of [things-in-themselves] that freedom is separated from and reunited to the end which it pursues, and which makes known to it what it is. Consequently, the resistance which freedom reveals is the existent, which far from being a danger to freedom, results only in enabling it to arise as freedom. There can be a free for-itself only as engaged in a resisting world.[30]

The significant difference between the views expressed in *Being and Nothingness* and the *Critique* in regard to the question of obstacles encountered in the world is that, in his later work, Sartre seems to be concerned with clearly identifiable, socially determined resistances or obstacles rather than with any possible obstacle man may encounter in his experience. He is no longer concerned with a description of *négatités* in general, but with discerning the most universal negativity which seems to be the origin of human misery and conflict amongst men. While there are counterfinalities which rebound upon human freedom (e.g., the pollution of rivers and streams by industrial waste), there is, in Sartre's view, one underlying negation which impinges upon man's freedom — that is *rareté* or scarcity. Sartre explicitly denies that man is free in all situations. Rather:

> ... we want to say exactly the opposite; namely that all men are slaves insofar as their vital experience takes place in the field of the practico-inert and in the exact measure in which this field is originally conditioned by scarcity.[31]

---

30. *L'Être et le néant*, p. 562.
31. *CRD, p. 369*.

Although this negativity is sometimes given a purely material basis, Sartre also argues that the social dimensions of such a limitation on man's freedom are equally significant. The antidialectical power of the practico-inert is often generated by, or sustained by, social institutions or the interests of certain social groups. Insofar as men interiorize antidialectical negations, they have an impact on the forms of social life. As is implicit in Marx's understanding of the condition of man, it is assumed that the material conditions of life determine modes of production which, in turn, determine social relations. Therefore, the problem of scarcity is construed, for the most part, as a social problem and not solely as an antidialectic which is an inert, material factor undermining the free, projective activities of men. As Sartre expresses it:

> ... it is ... scarcity ... as a real and perpetual tension between man and his environment, between man and man which, *for all intents and purposes,* accounts for our fundamental structures (technology and institutions): not because it would have produced them as an actual force, but because they have been established in a *climate of scarcity* by men whose *praxis* interiorizes this very scarcity in its efforts to overcome it.[32]

For Sartre, it is the social determinations which are inherited from previous socio-political institutions or social practices which are the most significant causal factors which work against the projects of individuals or groups. In one sense, it is still maintained that, in the final analysis, it is "the other" as a social being who is the primary threat to my freedom. However, in the *Critique* a sociological analysis of the other (whether as individual or member of a group) is given precedence over the previous psychological analysis of the relationship between oneself and the other. The other is now seen as an actual or potential negation of my freedom or, for that matter, my existence itself by virtue of his *praxis* within a *milieu* of scarcity. It is the existence of the hostile others which is the most universal source of the inhibition of the realizations of free projects which aim at the transcendence of social or material conditions which are obstacles to the liberation of individuals. In this regard, *praxis* is described as an:

> ... organizing project going beyond material conditions towards an objective, and imprinting itself through work in inorganic matter as a reworking of the practical field and reunification of the means with a view to attaining the end.[33]

The inert, material resistances which are to be surpassed include both actual environmental factors (which, as in the case of the Eskimo peoples,

---

32. *Ibid.,* pp. 203-204.
33. *Ibid.,* p. 687.

may be incapable of transformation or modification) and social groups or institutions which may have acquired inertial characteristics which convert them into entities which appear to be *inorganique*. Such antidialectical social phenomena are emergent and contingent (in the sense of being nonnecessary) in much the same way as are Gurvitch's "partial determinisms." The dynamic processes of the reciprocities of social existence invariably include emergent negations of individual projects which are themselves blocked by the projects of others (specifically, other groups). In this respect, Sartre — like Gurvitch — admits a dimension of social determinism over and above the material, causal factors impinging upon the existence of individuals. What Sartre describes as the univocal relation of the material environment to individuals is manifested in man's history. It appears under specific and contingent form in all human enterprizes as a fierce struggle against scarcity.

The dialectical processes assumed to be immanent in social existence reveal, at various stages, both the contingency and necessity which characterizes individual *praxis* in a social *milieu*. From the interiority of subjective, intentional action to the exteriority of inert matter or the socially conditioned practico-inert there is a dialectical movement from individual projects through exterior obstacles to what Sartre describes as the interiorization of the exterior. The clearest example of this instance of dialectical relationships of reciprocity in social existence is the way in which man acts in order to overcome an experienced need *(besoin)* in such a way as to convert himself into a quasi-object which acts in a field of exteriority. Whether the individual engages in work (and thereby assumes an objective function identifiable by others) or becomes a member of a group, he is engaged in a process of objectification in the social world which has, as its subjective correlate, an accompanying activity of totalization. That is, action constitutes the surrounding material field as a passive totality. It is in the relation of interiority that the organism in need is united with an environment which can be acted upon to alleviate that need. In this sense man is the intersecting point of the organic and inorganic order. Human work is described as the original *praxis* of man and is the response of the individual to an experienced need or negation. The central characteristic of work is the way in which the organism (man) makes itself inert (or quasi-inorganic) in order to transform the inert environment.[34]

At one point, Sartre equates body, function, need and *praxis* in a questionable way. Although we might want to hold that there is an interrelationship amongst these, this casual equation of all of them is somewhat

---

34. *Ibid.*, p. 174.

arbitrary. For, it is the body (or, more accurately, the consciousness-body) which experiences need and the individual, *qua* body, functions in order to overcome or satisfy this need by virtue of intentional, projective action *(praxis)*. To my mind, one can describe this process in these terms (rather than in Sartre's paradoxical assertions) and still preserve the sense of his description of the generation of human action. At any rate, it is interesting to note the parallel with Sartre's earlier account of the origination of the projects of men. The "upsurge" of consciousness towards the realization of a project through concrete action is also accounted for in terms of a conception of consciousness as a lack. The transformation of Sartre's thought involves giving a more materialistic account of human need — e.g., it is said that human conflict occurs because there is not enough for everyone — and placing far more emphasis upon the importance of work. Sartre no longer seems concerned with the perpetual lack or negativity of consciousness as such, but with organic, material needs which presumably can be satisfied in a particular social order.

The relation between man and man is one which takes place in concrete social circumstances and conditions which are historical. These historical relationships are considered as the dialectical consequences of *praxis* or the multiplicity of activities which are manifested in a field of action. These activities, however, take place in an already constituted sociomaterial milieu and are subject to determinations of "exteriority." This account of the social determinism affecting individual existence (with the exception of a dialectical analysis) was already implicit in Sartre's description, in *Being and Nothingness,* of the "we-subject." However, it is argued in the *Critique* that there is the possibility of "being-with" *(Mitsein)* others as well as the familiar antagonistic relation with others (who are now considered as subjective agents) who are "not my reality." Clearly, action brings man into a materio-social domain in which subjective interiority must be exteriorized in order to attain its end or goal. The quantitative aspect of exteriority includes the individual's objective being-for-others. One realizes the determining action of the other insofar as his movement towards an end may be discovered in one's own movement towards an end. The objectivity of the social self is shown by virtue of the mutual constitution of others as instruments for the realization of one's ends and oneself as an instrument for the realization of the ends of others.[35] The intersection of dialectical social lines of reciprocal constitution is not characterized by totalization (or synthetic unification) except by the introduction of "the third" or the other for whom the relation between individuals is an objec-

---

35. *Ibid.,* p. 192.

tive relation. This description is but another strand of continuity with Sartre's earlier analysis of being-for-others. The difference between his sociological description and his phenomenological description on this issue is that the mutual dialectical relationship between subject and other is made explicit and is characterized as a lived dialectic.

In the complex description of the dialectic of *praxis*, we can discern the action and reaction, movement and countermovement in social processes which is characteristic of any dialectical sociological method. Although it is, in one sense, correct to characterize the reciprocity Sartre describes as "a principle of the contingence of a plurality of subjects,"[36] it is clear that the objectification of the individual entails a submission to an external "circle of conditions." As Sartre expresses it, a

... negative element of mechanical exteriority ... in the framework of a given society, always conditions the ... relation of reciprocity.[37]

Reciprocal relations between individuals (e.g., dyadic relations) are characterized by a dialectical tension which is mediated by "the third" which crystallizes these relations in a "living totality" which includes individuals, material worked upon and instrumental objects. Individual reciprocities are part of a larger, transcendent process which encompasses particular ends in a series of "global relations." This diffused or dispersed unity constitutes the social existence of dyadic reciprocities as functional elements in a larger totality. It is quite clear that Sartre describes this initial form of social relationship as a deindividuating condition in which each individual is an anonymous social being who, nevertheless, retains a subjective and interior sense of his own individuality. This state or condition is obviously one in which a plurality of individuals have lost a high degree of freedom. While this is only a stage in social existence, it is one in which exteriority functions as a negation of free individual practice. To be sure, it is a condition of temporary and partial determination; but it is a situation involving an atomistic dispersion which Sartre, at times, equates with molecular dispersion. One thing is clear: Sartre has abandoned his emphasis upon the absolute freedom of man (as consciousness) insofar as he considers man in a socio-material milieu. The complex network of dialectical relations is characterized (as in Gurvitch's sociology) by a circularity of conditioning factors, partial determinations and a *dialectique de l'action* which manifests itself in work. The residual question that remains in regard to the intelligibility of the "dialectic of *praxis*" is the possibility of a specific form of dialectical reasoning.

---

36. Klaus Hartmann, *Sartres Sozialphilosophie*, Berlin, 1966, p. 83.
37. *CRD*, p. 198.

Dialectical Reason

Although Sartre concedes that analytical reason is appropriate to an understanding of social phenomena and is, in fact, a stage in the dialectical understanding of concrete social processes, he is concerned with a consideration of the possibility of a type of reason which surpasses every other type of reasoning. Throughout the *Critique* Sartre makes reference to the hypothetical possibility of dialectical reasoning even though he occasionally appeals to it in an assertoric tone. The key to an understanding of the speculative exploration of the possibility of, or limits of, a dialectical form of reasoning is Sartre's assumption concerning the nature of dialectical *experience*. For, he argues that "dialectical consciousness is in fact consciousness of the dialectic" conceived of as a "movement" in objects and in human action.

The development of a critical dialectic which is opposed to the dogmatic dialectic of Marxism is deliberately initiated in a paradoxical way. One can engage in a critique of dialectical reason only through dialectical reason itself. However, this involves letting dialectical reason found itself and develop itself as a free critique of itself and as a movement of history and of consciousness itself. In effect, Sartre recognizes the circularity of the enterprize of establishing a transcendental justification of dialectical reason. To my mind, he is never successful in justifying a distinctive form of dialectical reasoning. For, in the final analysis, dialectical thought is reducible to a "lived," selfconscious dialectical experience. Consciousness in general is said to involve a certain relation of man to the world which surrounds him. In agreement with critics of Engels' conception of a dialectic of nature (e.g., Lukács), Sartre claims that if there is a form of dialectical reasoning, it applies solely to the social and historic world. Such a mode of reasoning would discover itself and found itself in and through the concrete action of men who are situated in a certain society at a certain stage of development.[38] This notion is closely associated with Sartre's sympathy with a slightly modified form of historical materialism. As a social agent, as a being capable of modifying his environment, man is clearly an *être matériel* who finds himself subject to other material processes that act upon him. If there is a "law" governing a historical materialism, this is itself a pervasive dialectic. The question that underlies Sartre's search for a form of dialectical reason is, under what conditions is a dialectic able to be founded? To some extent, he has already anticipated his answer to this question insofar as he agrees with Gurvitch that a hyperempiricism pushed

---

38. *Ibid.*, p. 129.

to its limits will disclose the dialectical nature of man's socio-historical experiences. Sartre's approach to this question proceeds from an analysis of man's practical experiences in their most ordinary form (i.e., work) to the hypothetical assumption of a mode of dialectical reason which makes the dialectical nature of that experience intelligible to us. At best, he only assumes the possibility of establishing the heuristic value of the notion of dialectical reason. The "apodictic experience" upon which he will base his theory is that of man in society and in history.

For Sartre, dialectical processes can be understood "from within," from a personal and subjective perspective which has an objective pole in the world. One does not seek to discover a dialectic in experience on the basis of *a priori* principles, but on the basis of lived-experience itself. We recognize here Sartre's previous approach to phenomenological description. That is, the emphasis upon the "how" of individual experience which leads to transindividual structures of human experience itself. As contrasted to the linear development of analytical thought, dialectical reasoning is cyclical and is sensitive to paradoxical assertions. Analytical reason is clearly appropriate to domains in which there are external relations. The complex is broken down into the simple elements out of which it is ostensibly composed. In analytical reasoning dynamic relations or processes are converted into static logical forms in order that they be elucidated. Analytical thought in its positivistic expression is reductionistic. Sartre believes that the primary stumbling-block for analytical reasoning is irreducible novelty, the emergence of "the new" cannot be explained in terms of known facts.[39] Insofar as analytical thought quantifies itself (or expresses itself in quantitative form) it is analogous to the process of objectification which Sartre believes is typical of "the practical organism" in general. In this sense, it is incorporated into Sartre's thought as a "practical moment of dialectical reason." What Sartre suggests is that analytical reasoning is a form (perhaps an inevitable form) of *praxis* which is an expression of a stage of dialectical reasoning. In order to illustrate the plausibility of the existence of dialectical reasoning (as distinct from analytical reasoning) he does not describe the nature of dialectical thinking as distinguishable from inductive or deductive reasoning, but, rather, appeals to the nature of human experience in its actuality. That is, he tries to persuade us of the dialectical nature of human *praxis* or of the immanent dialectical form of the totalizing activity of individual agents. Analytical thought seems appropriate to an understanding of a mechanical order, to phenomena conceived of as determinate things. Dynamic social or historical experience

---

39. *Ibid.*, p. 147.

seems to have its own appropriate mode of *compréhension*, an understanding "from within" the interior perspective of lived experience. Sartre desires to show that in concrete reality "the dialectical method is not distinguishable from the dialectical movement."[40]

The reality of the dialectical movement is, at first, a *consequence* of a multiplicity of concrete totalizations in the social world *across* a material realm. It is a "living logic of action" which is discovered precisely in the intelligibility of *praxis*. Dialectical processes are created anew through intentional action and are expressed theoretically when they are seen as transparent to self-reflective agents. Dialectical reason is presumably manifested in the totalizing or synthesizing activities of individuals seeking to realize their projects in a world. The dialectical process as a whole is not present to anyone since no one stands outside the totalization *en cours*. Recognition of the movement of dialectic in the socio-historical world is complicated by the fact that the very experience of the dialectic is itself dialectical. As the rationality of action, dialectical reason is itself nothing other than the movement of totalization itself. The consciousness of the dialectical process of action is a moment in the synthesizing or totalizing activity of individuals. So far, then, Sartre has so described *praxis* and the intentional activity of totalization that they are necessarily imbued with a dialectical form.

The immanent dialectical movement is described as a "singularized universal" or, in Hegel's terms, a concrete universal. It is singular insofar as it is manifested in particular circumstances, under particular conditions, and in the singular course of individual lives. It is universal in the sense that its particular expressions give rise to principles and laws of intelligibility which can be applied to similar phenomena. "Dialectical bonds" or relationships are said to be produced by the "movement of dialectical reason" (if it exists). Although this sounds as though Sartre has hypostasized dialectical reason, this is misleading. For, what he is concerned to argue is that dialectical reason is immanent in totalizing activity and in practice and is a "movement" which pervades socio-material relations if we but examined them in detail or in terms of their structures. Dialectical reasoning is never purely contemplative. Structures, relations and significations not accessible to analytical reason must be revealed in order to substantiate the notion of an intelligibility in the socio-historical world which is accessible to dialectical reason alone.[41] If there is a dialectical reason or, more precisely, a dialectical rational *praxis*, then it is necessary that it define itself as the intelligibility of "irreducible novelty" insofar as it is such.

---
40. *Ibid.*, p. 132.
41. *Ibid.*, p. 147.

Paraphrasing what he says about nothingness in *Being and Nothingness,* Sartre remarks that "the new comes to the world through man." Man creates novelty through concrete action, sustains this creation through the reorganization of practical fields and brings it into existence through the "universal technique" of thought. Novelty is immediately intelligible in man's activity itself and is the essential characteristic of the dialectical reason which, for Sartre, is the possible unification of theory and practice promulgated by the Marxists. Human thought, insofar as it is genuine *praxis* or a moment of *praxis*, is primarily characterized as the intelligent grasp of the new. Dialectical reason is immanent in the action of *agents dialectiques* who create a dialectical process in a practical field and are subject to the dialectical relationships impinging upon their existence.

The two forms of dialectical movements in social existence and history are the "constituted dialectic" and the "constituting dialectic." The intelligibility of the former is based upon our understanding of the latter. Both comprise a dialectical circularity which characterizes action in society. Thus, for example, a loosely structured assembly (series) of individuals can produce a group and a group can produce a series. Or, again, the individual constitutes an assembly through his practice and the group constitutes the individual as a social or historical agent. An entire totalizing movement will be comprised of tensions, oppositions and interactions which illustrate dialectical experience. In the process of new social movements there can be discerned numerous relations sustained simultaneously by a constituting or determining dialectic and a constituted dialectic. Such is the abstract form of all significant social relationships. In general, then, dialectical reason may be defined as constituting and constituted reason applied to practical multiplicities. Sociological or historical totalizations or synthetic progressions are characterized by a dialectical tension of freedom and necessity, of spontaneous free *praxis* and a submission to an encompassing totalizing process into which social agents enter insofar as they work to achieve an end in the socio-material realm of "exteriority." From the perspective of each dialectical agent, his work involves an exteriorization (or objectification) of the interior and a corresponding interiorization of the exterior. This is the essential feature of dialectical experience.[42] With the exception of the intentionality of the individual's *praxis,* dialectical experience is primarily a material process. That is to say that man acts in the world as a material agent or an "organic individual" in order to attain his projects. In work, he transforms matter into "worked upon matter" and is, in this sense, a productive agent. But transformed matter rebounds

---

42. *Ibid.,* p. 157.

upon man's free practice and limits or shapes his existence. This opposition is continually resolved and reborn in man's objectification of himself in society. Dialectical experience is this socio-material dialectical process.

Returning to the notion of *compréhension* he had introduced in the *Questions de méthode*, Sartre practically equates it with what he has called dialectical reason. For, understanding or *compréhension* is described as the translucidity of *praxis* to itself. Understanding, like Dilthey's *Verstehen*, is a form of reasoning appropriate only to *les sciences humaines* and is the practical agent's grasp of his action in the process of action itself (taking place within a totalization *en cours*). Sartre restricts comprehension to the intelligibility or rationality of *praxis* itself in order to avoid using it to refer to irrational intuition or sympathetic understanding. All intentional actions of individuals or of groups is accessible to *compréhension*. This follows from Sartre's earlier statement that *compréhension* provides the most viable access to a knowledge of purposeful human conduct. The dialectical relationship among human need, organic function and *praxis* is comprehensible because it is experienced dialectically. The fundamental material need of man reveals the most primitive dialectical characteristic of human existence insofar as it is a "negation of negation." That is, the experience of need "denounces itself" as a lack (*manque*) in the interior of the human organism. Whereas in *Being and Nothingness* Sartre held that the primary lack of human reality was consciousness or the "for-itself," he now claims that the primordial lack which man experiences is organic need. This indicates a primary shift in his thinking (previously mentioned) from a concern with abstract consciousness to a concern with the material and bodily existence of man in a socio-material world (mediated by others). This world is dialectical and the *praxis* which endeavors to surpass the inertia of the material or social world is also dialectical.

Building upon these descriptions, Sartre tries to present a social phenomenology of serialities, groups and organizations which reveals the universality of dialectical movements in society and in history. The condition for the possibility of dialectical reason, then, is the dialectical nature of man's critical or self-conscious social experience. Sartre's argument seems to have the following form: if a dialectical interpretation of individual or group *praxis* (and of the original dependent relationship of man upon the material world) is plausible, and if it is possible to grasp the complex reciprocity of social relationships and show their intelligibility, then dialectical reason is possible. Sartre is quite aware that he has not *demonstrated* the existence of something called dialectical reason. Rather, he attempts to persuade us that it is only dialectical reason - immanent in intentional *praxis* — which can comprehend novelty as novelty or follow the process of *dépassement* in totalizing activity. Any synthesizing comprehension of a process involving the paradoxical exteriorization of the interior *and* the interiorization of the exterior is a paradigm of dialectical thinking. In this regard, Sartre attempts to indicate the distinction between dialectical thinking and analytical thinking purely in terms of a way of thinking abstractly. This is quite unconvincing insofar as he does not show how our ability to understand opposing processes differs in any significant way from abstract thinking or reasoning in general. What he seems to say is that dialectical reasoning is, in fact, a unique way of *interpreting* phenomena which can also be subjected to the "atomistic" process of analytical reasoning. At no point in his discussion of dialectical reason does he show that its abstract employment differs from rational intuition or discursive reasoning in general. The very dialectical exposition of his own analysis of the "dialectic of *praxis*" is clearly accessible to what he calls analytical reason.

If, as Sartre says, "the principle of dialectical evidence must be the grasp of a *praxis* under way in the light of its end,"[43] he cannot indicate the distinction between dialectical and analytical reason in terms of a mode of reasoning or thinking insofar as analytical reasoning is a form of *praxis* in Sartre's view. All that Sartre manages to do is to suggest the heuristic value of a dialectical orientation toward social phenomena which does not require a unique form of reasoning, but indicates a plausible way of construing the complex relations manifested in social existence. The most plausible feature of Sartre's lengthy descriptions of *praxis* is his account of the dialectical form or nature of human *experience*. Apart from an exceedingly self-reflective and self-conscious social agent's *compréhension* of all of the ramifications of, and constitutive features of, his *praxis,* the notion of dialectical reason is practically empty. If Sartre's concept of *compréhension* (as a modified version of Dilthey's influential notion of *Verstehen*) serves the purpose which dialectical reason ostensibly serves, why is it necessary for Sartre to engage in a speculative exploration of the latter's possibility? To my mind, the key to an understanding of Sartre's concern with the possibility of a dialectical reason is his desire to present his own version of Hegel's "logic of contradiction." Although this entire issue is worth pursuing in greater detail, it would carry me far beyond my present concerns. It may be said, however, that it is Sartre's assumption (which follows that of orthodox Marxists) that there are "contradictions" in society and history which leads him to formulate a conception of dialectical reason.

---

43. *Ibid.*, p. 152n.

From a logical point of view, it is absurd to say that there are, in fact, *contradictions* in the socio-historical world. This is *a fortiori* the case if one is concerned with action or *praxis*. For, intentional action - overt action in the material world - cannot be contradictory. Either one acts or one does not. Either one performs *this* act or *that*. The notion of a contradictory action is simply absurd. What is indeed the case is that social and historical domains are comprised of contradictory tensions, oppositions, and conflicting projects which do produce oscillating waves of conflict. In the psychology of the individual, too, we find conflicting tendencies, desires, goals, etc. But such dialectical phenomena — or, more cautiously, phenomena which may be interpreted or construed *as* dialectical — quite clearly do not require a form of dialectical thinking in order to be rendered intelligible. Social and historical processes are complex and multidimensional, are characterized by conflicting movements, by contradictory tensions, by a "reciprocity of perspectives." And individual existence may be seen as a microcosmic mirror of similar processes. In this sense, Gurvitch's and Sartre's notion that social and historical processes are dialectical is persuasive. Certainly, Sartre's *Critique* is an heroic attempt to convince us of the dialectical *form* of human experience in the socio-historical world. What is characterized as a "dialectical nominalism" seems appropriate only to what has been called the *Realdialectik* or the specific dialectical movement in the realm of the socio-historical.[44] Sartre has not — despite his sophisticated arguments, illustrations and suggestions — validated dialectical reason in terms of showing the conditions for its possibility. What he has done is to attempt to fuse the abstract and the concrete, the general and the particular, in his account of *praxis* in order to illustrate his own understanding of what the unity of theory and practice would be like. The emphases upon the primacy of practice, the descriptions of human practice as dialectical in form, are persuasive and supported by a series of convincing presentations of the reciprocal relationships between the individual and the material world, the individual and others, the individual and groups and counter-groups. One can admit that there may be a "plurality of dialectical movements," dialectical agents, a dialectical relationship between human need and the exterior materio social world, or a social dialectic manifested in group-formations without assuming that there is a dialectical reason capable of understanding such processes. It is not dialectical reason which Sartre actually justifies in his social phenomenology, but, rather, "the dialectical structure of individual ac-

---

44. Klaus Hartmann, *op. cit.*, pp. 186-189.

tion" which he believes is the only basis for a historical dialectic.⁴⁵ Despite his intention, Sartre has not adequately provided a transcendental justification of dialectical interpretation of social processes and a social phenomenology which is, *mutatis mutandis*, a form of dialectical sociology. Gurvitch disagrees with Sartre primarily on the question of the initial, general orientation towards social existence. In his *Dialectique et Sociologie* Gurvitch remarks that Sartre is correct in holding that *les sciences humaines* (especially sociology) are in need of "the dialectic," but he is mistaken in assuming that they must be founded upon "a precise philosophical doctrine."⁴⁶

The question that is raised by the interaction of the thought of Gurvitch and Sartre is, do we discover the nature of human existence by virtue of an application of a dialectical method of interpretation to the phenomena of the "human sciences" or must we develop a philosophical anthropology which will illuminate the subject-matter of *les sciences humaine?* This question points back to a central concern of the philosophy of Dilthey, a concern with the creation of an *anthropologische Methode* which would elucidate the relationship between man's lived-experience and the socio-cultural and historical world. Sartre shares with Dilthey a concern with a practical empiricism, an orientation towards concrete phenomena, which has led him to seek an integration of philosophy, sociology and history under the guidance of a search for a philosophical anthropology. It is this project and not his sympathies with Marxism which pervades the dialectical explorations of the *Critique de la raison dialectique*. As Sartre expresses it in the conclusion of *Questions de Méthode:*

> In choosing as the object of our study, within the ontological sphere, that privileged existent which is man . . . it is evident that existentialism poses to itself the question of its fundamental relations with those disciplines which are grouped under the general heading of anthropology. And — although its field of application is theoretically larger — existentialism is anthropology too insofar as anthropology seeks to give itself a foundation . . . anthropology . . . implicitly demands to know what is the *being* of human reality.⁴⁷

Sartre's analysis of dialectical *praxis* as a form of practical reasoning is an attempt to contribute to an understanding of the existential situation of man in a social and historical milieu; that is, man's *compréhension* of

---

45. *CRD*, p. 279.
46. Georges Gurvitch, *Dialectique et Sociologie*, Paris, 1962, p. 171.
47. *CRD*, p. 104.

himself as a social or historical agent. But throughout his descriptions of man's dynamic "situation" in a social world he presupposes the dialectical form of social existence and convincingly shows the amenability of social processes to dialectical interpretation. It is his description of the dialectical nature of critical (self-reflective, self-conscious) social experience which has heuristic value and not the "dialectical reason" that is ostensibly operative in human *praxis*. That it is Sartre's description of an empirical social dialectic (elements of which are necessarily expressed in abstract terms) which is the only viable contribution to a general anthropology is indicated by the absence of any statement of dialectical principles or laws. It is Sartre's emphasis upon concrete (if occasionally hypothetical) descriptions and nominalistic classifications which precludes a formulation of dialectical principles. He does not succeed in describing a unique form of dialectical reasoning or in formulating dialectical principles because he is primarily concerned with describing what he believes is an immanent dialectical movement in society or in history which can be understood "from within" or as it is "lived" by historical individuals. Although it is theoretically necessary for his explication of his theory of social existence, it is doubtful that the ideal type of rational, self-conscious social agents he describes are anything other than theoretical fictions. Some of the consequences of this idealization of social agents will be explored in my concluding discussion of Sartre's theory of group-formation. Before turning to that discussion, it is appropriate to consider, *en passant,* some general features of Sartre's concept of social phenomena.

Social Phenomena

The phenomenological description of the dialectic of *praxis* developed in the *Critique* is opposed to the notion that the dialectic is reducible to the general laws of natural history or of social history. Engels' concept of a "dialectic of nature" is described by Sartre as an unjustified metaphysical hypothesis which has tended to support a "dogmatic dialectic" which has come to dominate Marxist thought. Although Sartre admits that it is logically possible that physio-chemical processes may "express a dialectical reason," he tends to say that dialectical relations are immanent only in the humanized world in which man lives. Basically, Sartre has not abandoned the phenomenological "appeal to what is directly revealed in conscious reflection as yielding greater certitude than any set, however internally consistent, of theoretical hypotheses."[48] The description of the

---
48. William McBride, "Jean-Paul Sartre: Man, Freedom and Praxis," in *Existential Philosophers,* ed. G. A. Schrader, New York, 1967, p. 278.

social world implies not only an intentional consciousness of that world (or its objects), but an interchange between man as an organic being and the material reality which he acts upon. A social phenomenology is concerned with a description of social phenomena as they appear to consciousness insofar as they are apprehended in the lived experience of social agents. Man as a social agent, "inscribes" his being on the materio-social world in which he acts.

As we have seen, the most fundamental dialectical interaction of man and the world is revealed in *besoin* or need. But even in this need-state the individual is able to relate himself to exteriority by virtue of his free consciousness. The negating function of consciousness described in *Being and Nothingness* is retained by Sartre in the *Critique* insofar as it is because of consciousness that there is a socio-material world. Man, as consciousness, is always other than the material world in which he finds himself. A material realm independent of the significations of man is never encountered by man. The empirical dialectic between man and the materio-social world is mediated by the "lived" body of man or what I have previously described as the consciousness-body. Since social phenomena are affected by human *praxis,* social phenomena are never encountered as purely objective entities. The practical field of "instrumental possibilities" in which social agents act is constituted by consciousness, by intentional projects and by "the rationality of *praxis.*"

As Gilbert Varet pointed out in his study of Sartre's earlier phenomenological ontology, the "reflective method" of *Being and Nothingness* is presented in an entirely dialectical form and the entire phenomenology is carried forward by a movement of progressive synthesis.[49] In addition, it is said that Sartre's phenomenological method reveals a movement construed in terms of "the rhythm of a continuous antithesis between the relation of exteriority and of interiority." These relations are precisely those disclosed in the phenomenology of the dialectic of social existence. The interiorization of the exterior and the exteriorization of the interior — the dialectic of the subjective and the objective — which is described as paradigmatic of critical social experience is an amplification of relations previously described in *Being and Nothingness.* In this sense, there is a real continuity between Sartre's phenomenological ontology of human reality as such and his phenomenological ontology of the social world. It is his own conception of phenomenology in association with Gurvitch's dialectical hyperempiricism which shapes Sartre's conception of the nature of social phenomena.

Prior to the development of his social phenomenology Sartre had

---

49. Gilbert Varet, *L'Ontologie de Sartre*, Paris, 1948, pp. 158-159.

come to accept the Marxian notion of historical materialism. In *Qu' est-ce que la littérature* (1947), he had said that the human enterprize is characterized by the polarities of success and failure. What was needed for an understanding of history — which is neither wholly subjective nor wholly objective — was a kind of anti-dialectic which is itself dialectic.[50] The project of the *Critique* had been germinating for some time before Sartre had attempted a phenomenological description of individual *praxis*, of the constituting dialectic and the constituted dialectic, of the activity of totalization, and the process of group-formation. In his prefatory essay "Marxism and Existentialism", he relates the aims of existentialism (specifically, Sartrean existentialism) and a Marxism transformed and revised by Sartre.

> Existentialism, like Marxism, addresses itself to experience in order to discover there concrete syntheses; it can conceive of these syntheses only within a moving, dialectical totalization which is nothing else but history.[51]

In the *Critique*, however, he only begins to approach the question of the nature of the universal totalization of history. For the most part, attention is given to the description of social processes (with some historical illustrations of the interpenetration of social processes and history) which include both a practical knowledge of things in concrete social situations where there is an interplay of objective factors and the subjective perspective which is a "moment in the objective process" in which there is an "interiorization of the exterior."[52] Sartre's actual method of description of social phenomena includes an objective description of hypothetical social relations which emerge out of individual *praxis* as well as a projective orientation which is similar (at least initially) to his earlier phenomenology of the world for consciousness. Social situations (like *situation* in general) are characterized by the interaction of the subjective and the objective in coordination with a notion of an immanent dialectical movement. This approach to the social world is tantamount to Gurvitch's dialectical hyperempiricism which ostensibly allows its "objects" to reveal the detailed structure of their movement. However, the objective features of the social milieu ultimately refer back to "a lived reality" which is capable of grasping the intelligibility of his action as it takes place. In intentional action the individual immediately encounters what Sartre describes as "collective objects" (or "totalities") which are given in their concrete materiality. These

---

50. J.P. Sartre, "Qu-est-ce que la littérature?" *Situations II*, Paris, 1947, p. 86.
51. *CRD*, p. 29.
52. *Ibid.*, p. 31n.

totalities are the common objects of daily experience — the newspaper I read, the office in which I work, the money used to purchase food, etc. The "reality" of such "detotalized totalities" is both contextual and referential (in the sense in which their *meaning* and value is determined by man). Social fields are "already constituted" by a host of significations which are cultural objects for members of a society. Man comes to understand himself as a social being in terms of his relationship to the totalities encountered in social fields. In critical experience there is a grasping of the intelligibility of a social field and one's action in it.

Throughout his discussion of the dialectic of *praxis,* Sartre presents a highly idealized portrait of an unusually self-conscious social agent. To my mind, the conception of social agents in the *Critique* is derived from an earlier notion of an ideal worker, despite the fact that Sartre denies he is writing solely from the perspective of the working class individual. What is said about the worker in "Materialism and Revolution" is entirely consistent with Sartre's description of the man of *praxis* in the *Critique*. For, he had said that:

> ... what [a worker] becomes aware of, in the course of action itself, is that he surpasses the present state of matter by a precise plan of disposing it in such and such a way; and since this plan is nothing but the arrangement of means in view of ends, he succeeds in fact in redisposing it as he has wished.[53]

This model of a self-conscious, somewhat philosophical "worker" is one which dominates the pages of the *Critique*. Concrete action is depicted along the lines of the behavior of the man of action despite occasional references to perceptual experiences of social phenomena which could be had by any individual. Sartre echoes his earlier description of the "worker" who surpasses and transforms the materiosocial world when he asserts that:

> Man defines himself by his project. This material being perpetually goes beyond the condition which is made for him; reveals and determines his situations by transcending it in order to objectify himself — by work, action, or gesture.[54]

Because of this type of model of a social agent engaged in "surpassing" the inertial social or material phenomena in the world Sartre's social phenomenology is something of a distortion of a purely descriptive sociology. In addition, it leads him to ascribe a rationality and self-consciousness to social agents which is quite unconvincing. In many respects, it is for this reason that (despite his intention to show the multidimensional character

---

53. J.-P. Sartre, "Matérialisme et révolution," *Situations II*, Paris, 1949, p. 204.
54. *CRD*, p. 95.

of social reality) there is a certain one-dimensional image of man's social existence in the *Critique*. From the standpoint of sociological thought, Sartre's social phenomenology is clearly dominated by a conflict paradigm of social relations. In this regard, I shall try to indicate (in my discussion of the theory of group dynamics) that Sartre's social phenomenology has an implicit *prescriptive component,* as well as being a hyper-rationalistic account of social behavior.

In his analysis of the encounter with social phenomena Sartre has not changed his mind about the basic form of man's concrete relations to others or to objects in the world since *Being and Nothingness*. For, he had described beings-in-themselves as brute obstacles to be overcome by man's concrete free action and had described others as alienating realities encountered in a threatening world. The significant shift of emphasis, as we have seen, is from a description of the world for an isolated consciousness to the situating of man as a bodily or material entity in a quantitative world of exteriority. This emphasis is, of course, already implicit in the description of man in concrete situation in *Being and Nothingness*.

Given the residual presence of his phenomenological ontology in his social phenomenology, it may be said that Sartre conceives of social facts in such a way that they coincide with his ontological schema. In seeking to show how his own philosophy of human reality is consistent with Marxism, he remarks that:

> Existentialism, too, wants to situate man in his class and in the conflicts which oppose him to other classes, starting with the mode and the relations of production. But it can approach this "situation" in terms of *existence* . . . it wants to reintroduce the unsurpassable singularity of the human adventure.[55]

Man's comprehension of the social fields in which he acts is determined by his existence, in reference to his projects, his acts of totalization. Social phenomena are created and sustained by *praxis* and are transformed by human action. By a process of "transubstantiation," human projects take on the characteristics of things without losing their original qualities. In work or *praxis* man, in a sense, becomes a "thing" or object and transforms the material phenomena acted upon into humanized objects. Thus, it can be said that anything man acts upon or any obstacle he attempts to "surpass" is thereby a *social* phenomenon. For Sartre, the priority of *praxis* is intimately associated with the priority of social existence. To my mind, this general conception of man's existence in the social

---

55. *Ibid.*, p. 108.

world has its origin in the early Marx's view that man is both a product of, and creator of, society. As Marx expresses it,

The individual *is the social being.* The manifestation of his life — even when it does not appear directly in the form of a *communal* manifestation, accomplished in association with other men — is . . . a manifestation and affirmation of *social life* . . . Though man is a *unique* individual — and it is just his particularity which makes him . . . a really *individual* communal being — he is equally . . . the ideal whole, the subjective existence of society as thought and experienced.[56]

The phenomenological description of the initiation of action in terms of the interiorization of an exterior negation that is need is not a description which differs from an earlier ontological assumption that "action necessarily implies as its condition the recognition of . . . an objective lack or, again, of a negativity."[57] The assumption that scarcity is the motivating factor of all *praxis* is empirically and historically false. Furthermore, the ostensibly primary social fact about man (that he acts in order to overcome the negation of a lack) seems to conflict with the notion that individuals enter a social milieu that is already constituted, already filled, as it were, by functional "totalities." For, such social phenomena do not indicate, by any means, an individual interiorization of objective lack experienced as need. Clearly, wealth and abundance generate more individual and organized *praxis* than scarcity. To take Sartre's initial assumption about the dialectic of *praxis* seriously would mean that there would be no true action without the "interiorization" of scarcity or a material lack. To be sure, Sartre is correct in holding that the primary needs of man reveal a dependency of the organic being on inorganic being. But it does not indicate a "primary contradiction of the organic and the inorganic."[58] If it reveals anything, it is simply man's causal dependence upon the natural world for his survival. The primary relationship between an individual incapable of satisfying basic needs (i.e., an infant) and others is one of complete dependence.

The negation (in Sartre's Hegelian language) of the most primitive negation experienced by man is accomplished by other human beings who already exist and function in a society. In order for man to exist as man, he must experience a dependent relationship to organic, and not only inorganic, beings. Although Sartre concedes that the relation between a man-

---

56. Karl Marx, *Economic and Philosophic Manuscripts of 1844,* trans. M. Milligan, New York, 1964, p. 130.
57. J.-P. Sartre, *L'Être et le néant,* p. 508.
58. *CRD,* p. 166.

in-need and the inorganic environment is an abstraction in the sense that it is human relations which mediate a material field, a significant phenomenological insight is obscured here. For, it is obvious that the most basic need-states of individuals require a social involvement for their satisfaction. The dependence of the neonate on others for the satisfaction of basic needs is the primary *social* experience of man even if it occurs prior to the sense of an I. The individual can only develop in a human community in an original dependent relation to others. It has been suggested that the child originally participates in the unity of a "we-experience" which is the primary form of contact with fellowmen.[59] Sartre avers that at a moment of "the dialectic," relations between men are conditioned by the inhuman (or the inorganic). Despite the validity of this claim, it is also the case that simultaneous with this process is man's passive dependence on the other. What this means, in Sartre's terms, is that the basic needs of man are not "negated" by an individual's action, but by a social bond of passivity. The primordial point of departure for man's social existence is not *praxis,* but *passivus* or *pathos* (in the sense of passively undergoing something). It is man's physical and psychological dependency needs which make him a social being.

Man, as an organic being, is not related to a material world by means of a "totalization" of a field of *praxis;* his most immediate relationship to a socio-material world is characterized by passive dependency. In Sartre's terms, man in need or in a state of dependency on others (and an environment) resembles a "passive totality." By means of a process of physical, emotional, intellectual and social development the individual becomes capable of surpassing his previous condition, as well as the inertia of the materio-social world. If Sartre desires to give an empirically rooted account of the "dialectic" of social existence, he cannot forego an analysis of the difficult process of individual development (or maturation) prior to the emergence of a full capacity for rational, intentional *praxis.* To be sure, he does mention, in passing, that the "surpassing" of one's own past is a long and difficult process.[60] Given that he illustrates his discussion of the development of life in "spirals" by references to the life of Flaubert, we may look to his most recent work — *L'Idiot de la famille; Gustave Flaubert, 1821-1857* — for a phenomenology of the dialectic of the life of a "bourgeois individual" which, to some extent, is anticipated in his essay on

---

59. Cf. Heinz Remplein, *Die seelische Entwicklung des Menschen im Kindes — und Jungendalter,* Munich, 1966, p. 184. Cf. also: Stephan Strasser, *The Idea of Dialogal Phenomenology,* Pittsburgh, 1969, Chapter Four, "The Growth of Awareness."
60. *CRD,* p. 71.

"The Progressive-Regressive Method." The analysis of the origination of social *praxis* in the *Critique* points back to prior conditions of existence which are mentioned briefly in Sartre's prefatory essay. The following remarks indicate that, at the time of writing the *Critique*, Sartre was quite aware of the lacuna in his phenomenology of the origination of *praxis* that I have pointed out. For, he asserts that:

> The given which we surpass at every instant by the simple fact of living it, is not restricted to the material conditions of our existence; we must include in it . . . our own childhood. What was once both a vague comprehension of our class, of our social conditioning by way of the family group, and a blind going beyond, an awkward effort to wrench ourselves away from all this, at last ends up inscribed in us in the form of character.[61]

It is not only our productive capacity which shapes our understanding of ourselves as social agents, but our own psychological individuality as well. But the realization of personal, existential projects in the world is expressed in a dialectic of *praxis* which involves us in an exterior world of socio-material forces. The man of *praxis* is subject to the efficacy of social facts, as well as being the creator of new social facts. Sartre conceives of social facts as things (as Durkheim did) and (as Weber did) not as things. That is, he adopts the paradoxical view that social facts are things in the sense that all things — directly or indirectly — are social facts. The reason why he adopts such an understanding of the factual nature of social phenomena is his insistence that "things are human in the exact measure in which men are things."[62] The social field as the place of interaction of the subjective and the objective, the active and the inert, the organic and the inorganic is comprised of "things" which are subject to quantitative analysis, but which are transformed into social phenomena through the action of man. There are "things" or "material objects" only insofar as there is man. Since a social field is comprised of "collective objects," things or material objects, the social facts that occur in such a field are "things" subject to causal and dialectical processes. On the other hand, human projects, "the teleology of human action," human significations imbue "things" with social meaning. The material world is humanized through the thought, experience and action of man. Reiterating what he said in *Being and Nothingness*, Sartre remarks that "in the human world all is human."

Insofar as social facts occur in the quantitative realm of exteriority, they are things (or may be construed as things). But insofar as man acts

---

61. *Ibid.*, p. 68.
62. *Ibid.*, pp. 246-247.

upon, works upon, matter, it is encompassed in a social world in which human significations are ascribed to it. *Praxis* converts matter into an instrument for human ends and encompasses inorganic entities in a totalizing project. We have a *compréhension* of social facts or social phenomena insofar as they are "inscribed" with the signification of past *praxis,* are accessible in lived-experience, and are elements in a totalization in process. Although Sartre says that some social phenomena or "automations" may escape our understanding insofar as we encounter an "anti-dialectical" limit, his account of social processes is shot through with the assumption of their intelligibility. Even the notion of the "constituting dialectic" transforming itself into an *antidialectic* or a "dialectic of passivity" does not indicate a phenomenon which eludes our understanding. For, the *antidialectic* is the result of "a *praxis* returning against itself" which possesses its own kind of intelligibility which we can discover.[63] Just as Sartre assumes that all human conduct is, in principle, intelligible so, too, does he assume that social processes and social phenomena are, for the most part, intelligible.

Seen from the standpoint of the intentionality of *praxis,* the antidialectic is the rebound of man's activity back upon himself. In effect, it results in a counterfinality which negates or undermines previous intentions — e.g., the Chinese deforestation program which produced floods, the industrial waste which produces a dangerous pollution of the environment. Such contingent counterfinalities are social phenomena which seem to be immanent counterdialectical processes which ought to be included in the dialectical circle. From Sartre's point of view, however, everything is "antidialectical" which works against the original ends of groups or individuals. In this sense, social institutions which, in maturity, tend to undermine the original purposes of human agents are also antidialectical. The antidialectical social phenomena described by Sartre seem reminiscent of Marx's lament about the objective social relations which emerge out of the actual process of human life and become "forces" that acquire power over men.[64] Indeed, the *locus classicus* for the notion of counterfinalities seems to be the description in *The German Ideology* of

> This crystallization of social activity . . . this consolidation of what we ourselves produce into an objective power above us, growing out of control, thwarting our expectations, bringing to naught our calculations, is one of the chief factors in historical development up till now.[65]

---

63. *Ibid.,* p. 154.
64. K. Marx, "L Feuerbach," in *Marx-Engels Historisch Kritische Gesamtausgabe,* Berlin, 1932, 1/5, p. 537.
65. K. Marx, *The German Ideology,* ed. R. Pascal, New York, 1939, pp. 22-24.

Marx describes these counterintentional social processes as exemplifications of alienation. And Sartre, too, sees alienation no longer as an ontological characteristic of man as such, but as having its origin in society. While Sartre retains the notion of the "alienating reality of the other" presented in *Being and Nothingness*, he amplifies the scope of alienation by pointing to its appearance in institutions, serial social relations, in counterfinalities, in all of the manifestations of "the antidialectical." One of the outcomes of Sartre's complicated description of social phenomena is the paradoxical conclusion that it is the free projective *praxis* of men which creates the material and social forces that undermine, curtail or negate human freedom.

Before turning to a transitional discussion of the emergence of reciprocal relations among men as the foundation of collective social units, there is a background assumption found in the *Critique* which is relevant to my concern to show, wherever possible, the threads of continuity between Sartre as existential phenomenologist and Sartre as sociological phenomenologist. Throughout his discussion of practical fields unified by the totalizing acts of individuals or groups Sartre assumes a conception of social space which is practically the same as that assumed in *Being and Nothingness*. For, it is said that social fields are "lived" in terms of Lewin's conception of hodological space. Sartre assumes that the life-space in which man acts is comprised of an assembly of attracting or repelling vectors which are directed towards or away from certain objects. The lived-space in which an individual acts is a psychological field in which one sees a situational totality. Man is described as having an immanent dialectical relationship to social phenomena which appear in a number of possible "social fields." Practical knowledge of a situation presupposes an orientation in hodological space which illuminates "concrete totalities." Individual praxis unifies practical or social fields and reveals the practical field as a hodological space.[66] The "synthetic conduct" of individuals involves a unification (totalization) of a field of lived space in which there are movements towards objects or away from objects. In relation to projected goals, objects in one's social field are seen as instrumentalities for achieving ends or as obstacles to be surpassed. The objects encountered in our lived social experience are significations which are illuminated by the action of others or our own action (by contrast, Sartre says that the significations in concrete situations are "illuminated" by consciousness in *Being and Nothingness*) in a social space construed as the real space in which men act. This general conception of man's being-in-the-world in terms of an orientation

---

66. *CRD*, p. 97.

in hodological space indicates the continuity between Sartre's phenomenological psychology and his phenomenology of man's existence in a social field.

In moving from a consideration of the "dialectic of *praxis*" in a materio-social field, Sartre builds upon his phenomenology of others in order to show the reciprocal relationship amongst individuals and others. The primary reciprocal relationship has — as in *Being and Nothingness* — a "dyadic" form. The amplification of human relationships encompasses a host of relationships amongst "thirds." When one is objectively designated by individuals as "the other" (as one who belongs to another class, another profession, etc.) this designation is internalized insofar as one places oneself in an objective "milieu" in which two other persons may realize their mutual dependence outside oneself.[67] Whether one is actively engaged in realizing a project or is merely a spectator of the conduct (in Sartre's illustration, a summer visitor (*estivant*) observing the work of two other men who are separated by a wall) of others, one is involved directly or indirectly in a social field in which there are related "lines" of *praxis*. The significant difference between Sartre's account of the recognition of the other in the *Critique* and in *Being and Nothingness* is that in the former he understands the other as a social agent, and in the latter as an alienating conscious being.

Each individual is considered as a center of an alternative orientation towards the objective world. For Sartre, reciprocal and triadic relations are the basis of *all* social relations. A complete, coordinated reciprocity between men would be possible only in an ideal society. Despite the fact that Sartre holds that social existence (i.e., being in a practical field as an agent or a social phenomenon subject to the totalizations of others) is characterized by positive or negative reciprocity, his descriptions of relations between individuals are, for the most part, suffused by a basic antagonism. Although it is said that scarcity is the foundation for the antagonism amongst men, there is a sense in which Sartre's concept of projected totalization practically entails a conflict of interests among social agents. This is indicated by Sartre's view that cooperative reciprocity requires either that a person sees the other as a *means* to the realization of a project or sees him as the creator of a project for which one is a means. The unity of the reciprocity of two individuals requires the mediation of "the third man." The extended relations amongst a sequence of social agents (each of which may be a "third" for others) reveals a *réciprocité vécue* which is the basic component of social existence. As in *Being and*

---

67. *Ibid.*, p. 184.

Nothingness, the third individual is the origin of the constitution of small or large groups and a system of third men becomes a horizontal or vertical series of social relations. Although there may be reciprocal relations amongst a sequence of third men, there is ostensibly no reciprocal relation between the third man and a dyad. Although these complex social relations comprise the essential ingredients of the social world and entail metamorphoses which reveal the shifting, dynamic nature of social existence, Sartre's schema of reciprocal relations seems unduly abstract and incomplete in regard to the unifying mediation of "thirds."

Sartre claims that the third man observer of the reciprocity of two individuals changes this reciprocity insofar as the end of their rhythm of activity is now related to their performances (in a work situation) by the third man. This seems to obscure the well-known sociological observation that there is a positive response (typically) to the presence of an observer whose recording of performances tends to enhance such performances. This certainly seems to imply a reciprocity between the observer (a third) and others. The principle that social reality is an "indefinite multiplicity of reciprocities" seems to include the notion that the third man (though a mediator) is himself in reciprocal relations with others in a social milieu. Clearly, the dynamic system of mediated reciprocities is the basis for the emergence of loosely structured assemblies. A class, as a collectivity, is described as a "material thing" which is a kind of diffuse seriality. The microsociological interactions within social totalities are dialectical processes by which man is mediated by material things in the same measure in which things are mediated through men. This gives us a general understanding of Sartre's conception of the being of social phenomena: proceeding from an individual's relationship to an exterior material field (or a social practico-inert which is a kind of "thing"), we discover reciprocal relations with others *across* a material field or mediating third men; proceeding from individual, dyadic, triadic or collective *praxis* we discover a practico-material field.

Although the true reality "is the singular man in the social field," this "reality" acts within a complex reciprocity of human relations and material forces. Although the free *praxis* of the individual is presumably the foundation of socially significant action, once man acts in the world of exteriority he makes himself into a "quasi-object" in order to be effective. Insofar as this aspect of Sartre's social phenomenology is emphasized, there is a type of materialization in social action which naturally leads him to describe social phenomena as things. In the movement from individual *praxis* to organized *praxis*, we may say that some social phenomena take on an inorganic form in the sense that all exteriority has a *quantitatif* nature.

Sartre is careful to emphasize the dialectical form of this process by holding that "each element [in a social milieu] is linked to the other elements, but it is linked *from its place in the series and through its escaping liason with all* intermediate elements."⁶⁸ The action of the individual involves him in a complex network of socio-material relations in which there are constraints and exigencies which comprise *la réalité constante* of social existence.

The constant dynamic reality of society is comprised of inert matter, inert social entities (the practico-inert fields), individual and collective *praxis,* dyadic and triadic reciprocities, and a host of mediations. All social phenomena are "humanized" insofar as they are acted upon, lived from within or are instruments for the attainment of projects. A social world is an intermingling of the objective and the subjective, exteriority and interiority, the inert and the dynamic, the organic and the inorganic. The tension in social existence is comprised of the dialectical relationship between subjectivity and objectivity or the dual movement in which the interior is exteriorized and the exterior interiorized. Sartre would, no doubt, repudiate Gurvitch's suggestion that Sartre's understanding of society requires a recognition of a social reality which is "transubjective" and "transobjective."⁶⁹ For, a knowledge of such a "reality" would imply the possibility of transcending the standpoint of one's existential involvement in the totalizations in society and history.

In a strict sense, Sartre does not consistently hold that "there are only men and real relations between men" in society.⁷⁰ For, as we have seen, social reality is comprised of encounters with inertial, non-human entities in terms of man's *rapport à la Nature,* with quasi-inorganic social phenomena (the practico-inert), with practical totalities (instruments, tools, or cultural objects) and with a variety of obstacles. Despite the realist emphasis upon the independence of social phenomena, Sartre still retains the notion (expressed in *Being and Nothingness*) that "phenomena . . . cannot exist as phenomena without appearing to a consciousness." The social arena in which man acts is a humanized world constituted by the projects and *praxis* of men. Thus, despite the occasional suggestions of a monistic, materialistic conception of man's situation in the world, Sartre retains the basic notion that man humanizes what he acts upon and transforms the exterior world through his projects, actions,

---

68. *Ibid.*, pp. 327-328.
69. Georges Gurvitch, *Dialectique et Sociologie*, p. 207.
70. *CRD*, p. 55.

totalizations and values. The most significant and insurpassable dimension of human life is found in socio-historical existence. The practical world of social action may not have the lucidity which Sartre tends to ascribe to it, but his descriptions of the various stages of dialectical processes in society often reveal a plausible account of the complexity of our social existence. The irrational contingencies of social life, the stochastic pheomena which undermine social planning or social engineering receive insufficient recognition. Even antidialectical social forces or counterfinalities are dealt with as phenomena which are quite intelligible. In terms of his emphasis upon the rational teleology of individual or group *praxis,* his assumption of our capacity to penetrate the most complex social phenomena, Sartre presents what is predominantly a rationalistic dialectical sociology.

Since Sartre is concerned with man "in situation" in the *Critique,* it is not surprising to discover that man's existence in a spatio-temporal practical field is as a "material reality" which ascribes to material objects human functions and significations.[71] The individual or the group engaged in realizing projects through action attempts to surpass the passive unity of objects which determine the material circumstances in which man finds himself. This general conception does not entail the adoption of a new ontology of the materio-social condition of man (e.g., what Heidegger would call a "thing-ontology") which is alien to the earlier phenomenological ontology of Sartre. Rather, it involves the incorporation (with some modifications and shifts of emphasis) of that ontology as the theoretical basis of a social phenomenology. Thus, for example, it is clear that the concrete freedom of man "in situation" entails organic "being-in-the-world," that the concrete and contingent existence of man in the midst of the world is manifested through the bodily facticity of the individual in relation to what Sartre called (in *Being and Nothingness)* "an indefinite multiplicity of reciprocal relations." Man's engagement in the world reveals the coextensivity of his body with the world. The body (in *Being and Nothingness* and the *Critique)* is a "center of reference" which situates an individual in a world comprised of a multiplicity of instrumental complexes or "practical totalities." The *Critique,* as a social phenomenology, incorporates the analyses of bodily existence, being-in-the-world-in-the-presence-of-others, concrete relations with others, the existence of the third man and situational freedom which had been presented in *Being and Nothingness.* The phenomenological description of social processes and social phenomena in the *Critique* is pervaded by the ontological assump-

---

71. *Ibid.,* p. 248.

tions derived from *Being and Nothingness*. The latter are synthesized with a dialectical orientation toward social processes which is similar to that of a dialectical sociology which sought to preserve the reality of human freedom in the midst of a variety of emergent "social micro-determinisms" and "partial determinisms."

In his description of serialities, groups in fusion and organized groups Sartre extends his social phenomenology from the microsociological to the macrosociological. Despite the subtle analyses of the interior development of groups which Sartre provides, I believe that he neglects significant parameters which are relevant to a description of collective social processes. Sartre proceeds from a description of the dialectic of individual action to what he obviously conceives of as the most effective force in the social world — that is, the organized *praxis* of groups.

IV. A PHENOMENOLOGY OF SOCIAL RELATIONS

> Everywhere and always social man is inventive, creative; everywhere and always he is in thrall to his own achievements. Henri Lefebvre, *The Sociology of Marx.*

If Jean-Paul Sartre's *L'Être et le néant* was an attempt to provide a phenomenology of the modes of the *pour-soi* and the *en-soi*, consciousness and material entities, his *Critique de la raison dialectique* is an attempt to present a phenomenology of the interaction between individual *praxis* and groups and of the process of group formation. In his analysis of the dialectic of social relations, he is still, more or less, faithful to the method of phenomenology—that is, the attempt to describe, elucidate, and make manifest the essential structures present in phenomena, to describe what manifests itself *as* it manifests itself. In addition, he is concerned with an ambitious attempt to synthesize his own existential ontology with a revised Marxism. He claims that ultimately Marxism will incorporate and transcend existentialism even though, at present, it is necessary as a corrective to the dogmatic dialectical theory of contemporary Marxism. In effect, he maintains that Marxism has neglected the role the individual plays in history and has submitted itself to a mystical conception of history in terms of which individual *praxis* is negated and injustices are accepted as inevitable aspects of an all-encampassing material dialectic. In this analysis, I have not been primarily concerned with the larger issue of the relationship between Sartre's existentialism and Marxism. Rather, attention will be focused upon the nature of his phenomenological description of group dynamics, on the specific contribution his analysis of dialectical interaction makes to a sociology of groups. Critical emphasis will be placed upon three basic problems: (1) the conflict between Sartre's intention to preserve the importance of individual action and his description of the coercive power of groups and their transcendence of the individual; (2) the question of Sartre's interpretation of the dialectical process of group formation; (3) the general neglect of irrational factors which contribute to the formation, unification, and genesis of groups. A more general concern will be the apparent contradiction in Sartre's *Critique* between the contingency of individual action and the necessity which characterizes the nature and development of groups in his account. In regard to (3), an appeal will be made to some of the insights of Freud and Gustave Le Bon to undermine Sartre's confidence in the assumption that the phenomena of group dynamics are wholly intelligible and are characterized by conscious intentions or a rational teleology.

Critical Dialectic versus Dogmatic Dialectic

In order to understand why Sartre uses the descriptive terminology he does in his explication of the sociology of groups, some attention must be paid to his theoretical presuppositions. In the first place, he admits that he accepts Marx's general sociological principle that the modes of production of material life determine, in general, the development of social, political, and intellectual life.[1] This commitment has significant consequences for the way in which Sartre understands the motivation for group formation and the general basis for social action. That is, he will seek the concrete foundation of social relations in a 'material' or economic factor. Despite this agreement with Marxist sociology, Sartre does not accept the view that there is a dialectic in nature itself apart from the *Lebenswelt* of man. He charges that the assumption of an impersonal dialectical process in nature (the laws of which determine human action and, hence, history) is neither an empirical fact nor a 'law.' Rather, it is an unjustified metaphysical hypothesis.[2] Such a hypothesis is closely related to the view that historical events can be understood in terms of a universal dialectical determinism or in terms of a pervasive necessity. It entails the notion that the causal relations among natural and social events are characterized by necessity even though dialectical materialism postulates contradictions in nature and in society. Sartre opposes his own critical dialectic to what he calls the dogmatic dialectic of contemporary Marxism. A *dialectique critique* interprets human actions and history in terms of a dialectical process of reciprocal interaction between individual and individual, man and world, individual and group. Although human existence is obviously affected by the material conditions of life, man is not merely a passive victim of a dialectical process over which he has no control. If this were not the case, it would make no sense to speak of *human* history since all history, in a manner of speaking, would be *natural* history. Borrowing a Hegelian

---

1. *Critique de la raison dialectique*, p. 31.
2. *Ibid.*, p. 129.

term, Sartre claims that man is 'mediated' by things or objects in the same measure in which objects or things are themselves mediated by man.³ Although material objects and processes are encountered in themselves in their 'brute' facticity, they *are* in relation to human consciousness, in a field of instrumentality in which they are objects of the intentional consciousness of man. Following Husserl and Heidegger, Sartre maintains that the ontic phenomena man encounters are constituted by the intentional consciousness of man and have meaning in relation to man's modes of being, his concrete situation, and his projects. Objects for use (Heidegger's *zuhanden*) which have value or meaning have a relational mode of being in reference to a signifying being, man. For, it is through man that meaning is brought into the world.⁴ Insofar as man is *createur de signes*, he determines the significance of the facticity of objects and transcends this recognition by converting things into signs which become instruments of purpose by which he can project himself into the future and transform the phenomena he encounters.

When human understanding is linked to action, the 'movement' of man is progressive. Since man is defined in terms of his projects, the equipment he uses is mediated by his intentions. Sartre rejects the metaphysics of dialectical materialism because it cannot account for the free, creative practice of man. That is, he objects to Engel's interpretation of dialectical materialism insofar as it undermines the anthropological context of this theory as Marx originally formulated it and makes man subject to 'laws' which are conceived of as wholly outside himself. Against such a view Sartre argues that the "only practical and dialectical reality, the mover of everything, is *individual action*."⁵ Although the claim that man is the

---

3. *Ibid.*, p. 165: "La decouverte capitale de l'experience dialectique . . . c'est que l'homme est 'medie' par les choses dans la mesure meme ou les choses sont 'mediees' par l'homme."
4. *Ibid.*, p. 96. Cp. Martin Heidegger, *Sein und Zeit*, Tubingen, 1963, p. 151: "Wenn innerweltlich Seiendes mit dem Sein des Daseins entdeckt, das heisst zu Verstandnis gekommen ist, sagen wir, es hat Sinn."
5. *Ibid.*, p. 361. Cp. Karl Marx and F. Engels, *The German Ideology*, New York, 1947, pp. 6-7: "The premises from which we begin are not arbitrary ones . . . They are the real individuals, their activity and the material conditions under which they live, both those which they find already existing and those produced by their activity." Cp. also, the remark in *A Contribution to the Critique of Political Economy*, Chicago, 1904, p. 265: "Individuals producing in society, and therefore a socially determined production by individuals, naturally constitute the starting point." Recently, Adam Schaff has suggested that individualism and Marxism are compatible and has attributed a misunderstanding of Marx's views on this question to Marxist interpreters such as Lukács. For

mover of *everything* is a rather incredible exaggeration, Sartre intends to re-emphasize the humanistic standpoint of early Marxism and to insist that man, by virtue of his intentional action, is not entirely subject to forces beyond his control. The world, for Sartre, is a humanized world, one which is constituted by the consciousness, intentions, and projects of individuals. To be sure, matter is real and independent of human consciousness (the *en-soi* of *L'Être et le néant*), but the meaning and use of material objects or forces is constituted by the activity of individuals. Because of his stress upon the intentional consciousness of individuals, Sartre denies the universal presuppositions of the metaphysics of materialism.

In an earlier essay, *Materialisme et révolution,* Sartre had argued that materialism was a self-contradictory metaphysics which attempted to eliminate human subjectivity by converting man into an object. But instead of understanding man as an object moved by other objects, the materialist claims that he is an objective observer who can 'know' reality as a system of interrelated material objects or processes. Sartre asked: "How could a captive reason, governed from without, manoeuvered by a series of blind causes, still be reason?"[6] In his *Critique* he repeats this criticism and charges that dialectical materialism is negated by the assertion of its truth. If a man is immersed in material processes, if he is conditioned by an absolute dialectical movement which affects every aspect of his being, how can he be that 'consciousness' which is certain of its own existence and of the 'truth'?[7] We cannot understand the dynamics of social relationships unless we assume that the individual is the basis of the historical dialectic, that social actions are the result of human *praxis* which is manifested in a series of intelligible dialectical processes. Like the early Marx, Sartre maintains that the individual, though unique, is a social being, that thought and being are distinct though intimately interrelated and are both essen-

---

Schaff refers to Lukacs' assertion in *Geschichte und Klassenbewusstsein* that the "totality of the historical process" cannot be understood from the perspective of the isolated individual. Schaff contends that Lukacs draws the unjustified conclusion that there is no room, in Marxist thought, for the conception of the human individual. Against such an interpretation of Marx, Schaff points out that there is "an important part of individual life" which "is beyond the reach of such evaluations" insofar as it is "socially neutral." *Marxism and the Human Individual,* p. 53. Whether one is convinced by Schaff's understanding of Marxism or not, his is the most heroic attempt to defend the concept of individual existence in the framework of Marxism. In this sense, there are many affinities between Sartre's fusion of existentialism and Marxism and Schaff's liberal reinterpretation of Marx's thought.

6. J. P. Sartre, *Literary and Philosophical Essays,* p. 203.
7. *CRD,* p. 126.

tially activities.[8] Marx maintained that the significant 'Nature' for man is that which has developed throughout his history, in his societies; hence, it is truly "anthropological Nature."

If we are speaking about man as an historical being, we may say that such a being does not live in Nature in the same way in which an animal lives in a natural environment. For, his thought, language, and actions emerge within a social context which is "already there," already constituted — the dominant "nature" affecting an historical man's existence is a social world and the complex relationships which characterize it. It is Sartre's intention to trace the development of groups (or other collectivities) in order to elucidate the understanding of a concrete individual being, the historical man. The initial moment or stage of the social dialectic is discovered in individual *praxis*, a *praxis*, of course, which is only possible within the larger context of society. Sartre chooses this as a starting point for his social phenomenology because he holds that *"praxis"* is the measure of man and the foundation of truth."[9] Like the early Marx, Sartre conceives of *praxis* (Marx's *Tätigkeit*) as a general notion which includes the intentionality of consciousness, freely chosen projects, subjective teleology as well as overt physical activity or social action affecting material conditions of life.

Sartre adopts a dialectical approach to explicate social development because he is under the influence of dialectical sociology and because he believes that the analytical conception of man and his society makes man into a determinate object which can be classified, categorized, and understood in the same way in which a physical object is understood. An analytic interpretation of human being and action converts man into an abstraction (usually a statistical postulate) which is no longer a living entity whose existence is revealed in his becoming. The dynamic processus of the reciprocal interrelationship between man and environment, man and man, cannot be classified in terms of abstract notions appropriate to a description of

---

8. Karl Marx, *Economic and Philosophic Manuscripts of 1844*, pp. 104-105. This concept of the unity of "thought" and "being" is interpreted by Henri Lefebvre to mean that "praxis is the condition of real theory." It is assumed that the antinomies of philosophical reflection—subjectivity versus objectivity, spiritualism versus materialism and activity versus passivity—can only be resolved by concrete social action. Lefebvre maintains that Marxism "transcends" philosophy and does not entail a pragmatic orientation towards the world. Although Sartre's philosophy of praxis seems to be designed to overcome the antinomies of philosophy, it is clear that he understands Marxism as a philosophical perspective with a strong empirical and pragmatic emphasis. In this regard, Lefebvre's attempt — in *The Sociology of Marx* — to dephilosophize Marxism is quite questionable.
9. *CRD*, p. 741.

inert substances. Social reality is a complex, indefinite multiplicity of reciprocities.[10] Strictly speaking, these reciprocities are 'infinite' in the sense that the reciprocal causal interactions amongst social beings create new conditions which, in turn, generate other actions, reactions, or oppositions which are, in turn, affected by emergent social phenomena or changes in the material environment. In this sense, Sartre's social phenomenology is an attempt to describe the general ontological characteristics of group dynamics derived from ontic social phenomena which involves the selective apprehension of the complex reciprocity of social processes manifested in on-going processes which are indefinite.

A phenomenological approach to social phenomena is an interpretation (as Heidegger pointed out in *Sein und Zeit* there is no phenomenology without interpretation — *Auslegung*) of the essential structures manifested in such phenomena. It has been said that a purely naturalistic social science does not directly deal with the commonly shared social world as it is experienced "from within," but tends to treat human actions as mechanistic forces or is only concerned with the "behavioristic" aspects of human social relations. This naturalistic approach to social phenomena is apparently what Sartre means by the analytical orientation and which he identifies with Emile Durkheim's view that social facts are to be studied as are other natural phenomena.[11] Characteristically, Sartre adopts a paradoxical position in this regard. He claims that *les faits sociaux sont des choses dans la mesure où toutes les choses directement ou indirectement, sont des faits sociaux*. Although this statement is not clarified, it would seem that what is suggested is that "things" or objects are social facts in the sense that their signification or meaning is related to their function, use or role in a social *milieu* in which there are a multiplicity of significations which are dominant in social life. On the other hand, his own comments on the nature of social phenomena suggest that some social facts (the practico-inert) are "things" or inorganic entities and others are intentional processes *(praxis)*. Insofar as he seems to accept the notion of total social phenomena, Sartre does stress the priority of social facts in his analyses. In this sense, he seems to be maintaining that all things are, in the final analysis, *faits sociaux*.

Although Sartre concedes that some social phenomena are inert or subject to inertia, he insists that experience in itself, as it is experienced in its phenomenological diversity, is dialectical. That is, it is characterized by action and reaction, opposition, a dynamic interaction of social energies,

---

10. *Ibid.*, p. 197.
11. Emile Durkheim, *Les Règles de la méthode sociologique*, Paris, 1950, pp. 15, 27ff.

individual or collective. An analytical orientation toward social phenomena discovers only the quantitative aspects of these phenomena and tends to transform qualitative factors into a quantitative form. The attempt to provide formulae for the logical structure of social relations or social actions leads to such an abstract level of the relation of variables that such formulae are either reducible to tautologies or may be applied to such a large class of phenomena that we have no specific understanding of the social phenomena they ostensibly 'describe.' To say, as some quantitative social analysts have said, that the statement of a relation between variables must include an unmeasurable variable (a disturbance or stochastic relation) which is included in the formula depicting a social phenomenon (or process)[12] does not provide any more understanding of the nature or role of such disturbance factors than we had before. A phenomenological orientation toward social phenomena would attempt to discern the nature of such disturbance factors insofar as this is possible. In other words, it attempts to reach a level of specificity which is closed to a purely analytical approach. A social phenomenology is not only concerned with a description of the 'what' or the facticity of social relationships or social phenomena, but with the 'how' of the concrete experience of social action, social relations, and social phenomena in general. Analytical reason, Sartre avers, is a synthetic transformation which affects itself intentionally and is a mode of thinking which makes itself a thing *(cette pensée doit se faire chose)*.[13] It is a mode of reasoning appropriate to an understanding of a mechanical order *(ordre mecanique)* and not social phenomena which are emergent, novel, and contingent. Hence, Sartre adopts what he calls dialectical reason as a mode of thinking which is more appropriate to an understanding of social phenomena and which, although bearing an asymptotic relation to such phenomena, approximates the concrete and specific form of the phenomena it is concerned with in a phenomenological description.

The individual is able to discover and understand the dialectic of experience since he himself practices it.[14] That is, it is immanent in concrete experience and is the characteristic phenomenological structure of that

---

12. Kenneth J. Arrow, "Mathematical Models in the Social Sciences," in *Readings in the Philosophy of Social Science*, ed. M. Brodbeck, New York, 1968, p. 663.
13. *CRD*, p. 148. Sartre admits that analytical reasoning is a phase or stage in the process of dialectical thinking, but that it is one which must be surpassed in order to arrive at a comprehension of dynamic processes. In regard to this issue, there is an analogy between Gurvitch's critique of "abstract empiricism" and Sartre's criticism of the limitations of the use of analytical reasoning in sociological understanding.
14. *Ibid.*, p. 133.

experience. The dialectic is characterized as a "living logic of action" which manifests itself in and through the totalizing activity of the individual. The term totalization (which was used as early as 1843 by P. J. Proudhon in his *De la création de l'ordre dans l'humanité* and by Sartre in *L'Être et le néant*) refers to the process by which parts enter into social wholes, the synthetic unification of elements within rational totalities. Social totalities are held, by Sartre, to be the basis of all other totalities. The individual is conditioned dialectically by the past which totalizes the 'human adventure.' At the same time, as a man of culture (an expression which designates every man and not an elite intelligensia), the individual totalizes himself from an entire past. The individual invariably engages in the process of totalizing his experiences, understanding them as holistic structures, synthetic unities. The implication of this viewpoint, this emphasis upon the totalizing activity of man, is that the individual cannot escape history since he already exists within (and is constituted by) historical totalities. In all social experience there is a pervasive *nisus* towards totalization. Totalization or the totalizing intentional activity of the individual within the dialectic of experience always tends towards *praxis* or action and is never merely an act of contemplation.[15] Thus, the cognitive process of unification of diverse, but related, elements is an intentional activity of consciousness which is linked with teleologically determined practice. Like Hegel, Sartre insists that dialectical thinking is a mode of understanding processes, becoming, the dynamic interplay of oppositions, contradictions, the negations and syntheses which characterize existing beings. Unlike Hegel, however, he seems to hold that it is not thought which determines the nature of being (or that thought and being are inseparable), but that it is actuality — the concrete conditions of becoming — which determines thought. To put this another way, it may be said, for Sartre, that the dialectic of experience is existentially prior to the dialectic of thought. The dialectical *Existenz* of individuals is already there (pre-philosophically, pre-phenomenologically) before man reflects upon that existence, before he seeks a philosophical language by which he can make that experience intelligible to himself. At any rate, society is itself a totality-in-process which is, as it were, 'produced' by the multiplicity of practical relationships with others who are engaged in the totalization of their singular or particular experiences.

---

15. Cf. G. Lichtheim, "Sartre, Marxism and History," *History and Theory*, III, no. 2 (1963). This notion corresponds, more or less, to Sartre's early conception of practical consciousness or the non-positional, non-thetic consciousness of one who is engaged in an activity.

Scarcity, Action, and Group Formation

Totalization is an intentional act of consciousness directed towards some actual or possible action. It is not merely an act of speculative reflection concerned with hypothetical possibilities or theoretical synthesis; rather, it is a consciousness linked with what Marx called the life process of existence, reflection intimately associated with action. The process of totalization takes place within a field of totalities which are objects of reflective awareness. If, for example, I am a worker in a factory, the factory is a totality, and the tools or instruments I am using are totalities. My reflective awareness of being in a factory places my dialectical experience within the totalizing movement of which I myself am a part. That is, the individual is a significant 'moment' in the "totalization in process."[16] And the multiplicity of totalizing activities is itself the dialectical process of which the individual is already a 'part' or moment. The self-reflective consciousness of individuals enables them to recognize, analyze, interpret, and describe the existential dialectic of social experience which already conditions their thought about that experience. The task of a social phenomenology, then, is the elucidation of the essential structures and meanings of the existential dialectic of social relations and actions. The social existence of man is constituted by (a) the holistic totalizations *en cours* of which he is a part or element — e.g., the society in which he lives; (b) his own totalizing activity which organizes and synthesizes the diverse relata which he encounters in his experience; (c) the historical, material conditions of life which affect his mode of existence in general; and (d) the totalizing activity of other individuals or groups.

The individual's use of a totality (a stabilized instrumental entity constituted by a holistic interrelationship of parts or elements) is *praxis*. Sartre emphasizes *praxis* in order to express the interrelation of theory and practice in the Marxist interpretation of human experience and because of his commitment to the view expressed in *Being and Nothingness* — that *faire* or "doing" is one of the "cardinal categories of human reality." He had long been concerned to argue that man creates himself through action.

His early emphasis upon concrete action is clearly compatible with his conception of freedom insofar as the *pour-soi* or consciousness is engaged in situation. The world of brute facticity (the *en-soi*) limits our freedom of action even though it is human freedom (the freedom of consciousness) which constitutes the framework, the techniques, and the goals in terms of

---

16. *CRD*, p. 140.

which beings-in-themselves will show themselves as limits.[17] Consciousness determines the *meaning* of the obstacles (or brute facticities) it encounters though it does not (as in idealism) create such phenomena. All of this is quite compatible with Sartre's account of the relationship between consciousness and action in his *Critique*. Praxis is the result of freely chosen projects, a manifestation of human freedom within a limiting material and social matrix.

Man's immediate relationship to the material field (*champ matériel*) is revealed in human work, in the original *praxis* by which he produces the means by which he may satisfy his basic needs. Since the material milieu is the first or most fundamental totalization of human relations, it is not surprising that Sartre insists that man's immediate relationships to the material environment take place in the form of a relationship to a practical field (*champ pratique*). [18] In Heidegger's terms man does not encounter the material field merely as something present-at-hand *(vorhanden)*, but as comprised of equipment ready-to-hand *(zuhanden)*.[19] The practical field in which the individual exercises his *praxis* is already given, already constituted. And the social relations of men within a practical field are determined by the existing material conditions of life transformed by virtue of specific modes of production. It is for this reason that Sartre seeks a socio-economic factor as the underlying causal factor determining individual and collective action. For, he claims that scarcity dominates all *praxis* (*la rareté... domine toute la praxis.*)[20]

In assuming that the basic foundation of social development is the "fierce struggle against scarcity," Sartre seems to believe that he has presented a Marxist view. Although Marx is not entirely consistent on this question himself, he did not assume that scarcity was the movivating factor

---

17. *L'Etre et le néant*, p. 562.
18. *CRD*, p. 199.
19. Martin Heidegger, *Sein und Zeit*, p. 69. This pragmatic orientation towards a humanized world is a dominant practical mode of being of *Dasein* for Heidegger, one which is dominated by a "circumspective concern" for non-human entities in the world. Sartre's conception of a practical field resembles Heidegger's description of the practical world as a complex system of relationships and significations.
20. *CRD*, p. 206. The view that praxis is generated by a material lack or need such as scarcity is reminiscent of the early Marx's description of the fundamental condition of man. For, Marx had averred that man "as a natural, embodied, sentient, objective being ... is a suffering, conditioned and limited being ... The objects of his drives exist outside himself, as objects independent of him, yet they are *objects* of his *needs*, essential objects which are indispensable to the exercise and confirmation of his faculties." *Economic and Philosophic Manuscripts of 1844*, cited in Erich Fromm's *Marx's Concept of Man*, New York, 1961, pp. 181-182.

in social (and, hence, historical) evolution. At various times he attributes the dominant causal basis of social development to (1) greed,[21] (2) exploitation, and (3) class antagonism. In his *Economic and Philosophic Manuscripts* Marx charges that the political economists understand only one basis for economic development — competition or avaricious conflict. In the language he later uses, this means that such a factor ostensibly underlies modes of production and, hence, social relations and developments. Although Marx emphasized the exploitation of workers in his later criticisms of capitalist production, there is a residual sentiment that avarice is a motivating factor in such activities. His tirades against the drive to accumulate money in the manuscripts indicates that he seems to have believed that "greed" or the need to accumulate wealth is, indeed, a significant motive for social action in industrial or *capitalist* societies. Many of Sartre's rhetorical criticisms of capitalism and the "exploitation" by the French colonialists in the later portion of the *Critique* are reminiscent of the expressions of moral outrage of Marx.

In his work of 1847, *The Poverty of Philosophy*, he explicitly defends (3) — perhaps his most consistent position — as the basic source of social change:

> The very moment civilization begins, production begins to be founded on the antagonism of orders, estates, classes, and finally on the antagonism of accumulated labor and actual labor. No antagonism, no progress. This is the law that civilization has followed up to our days.[22]

It is on the question of the basic source of the antagonism between groups in society that Sartre seems to misunderstand a fundamental principle of Marxism which he is presumably expositing. For, as Adam Schaff has pointed out, it is not scarcity or a material lack which is assumed as a basis for social antagonisms in Marxist thought. Rather, as Schaff puts it,

> The Marxist conception of exploitation and surplus value is based on the fact that the worker produces *more* than the minimum amount required for his own satisfaction according to his historically determined living standards.[23]

---

21. Karl Marx, *op. cit.*, p. 68.
22. Karl Marx, *The Poverty of Philosophy*, p. 61.
23 Adam Schaff, "A Philosophy of Man," in *Existentialism versus Marxism*, p. 314. It should be noted that Henri Lefebvre does not seem to agree with Schaff on this point insofar as he holds that "Multiple conflicts are caused by the scarcity of goods, poverty, and bitter struggles over the tiny surplus of wealth produced." This scarcity, he claims, resulted from the appropriation of "social surplus" by "privileged groups" who solidified their grasp upon the wealth of the world by means of "ideology." Since this discussion occurs in the context of an exposition of Marx's understanding of the condition of the oppressed, we may assume that Lefebvre, like Sartre, believes that scarcity is a fundamental

Although Sartre may indeed be correct in assuming that some social movements, some group formations, come about as a result of scarcity under certain historical circumstances, it is an unjustified generalization to say that *all* social movements arise out of a struggle against scarcity. To be consistent with his own fundamental position he need only claim that individual *praxis* and the nisus towards the formation of groups takes place within an already constituted material field (strictly speaking, a practical field) which is dominated by specific material means of production. To say that human history develops in "the permanent framework of a field of tension engendered by scarcity"[24] is simply false. If we hold Sartre to what appears to be a secondary view — that human needs and the absence of the means by which to satisfy them are motivating factors in social movements —, then it may be admitted that the subjective experience of needs is a basic factor determining human action, work, and group developments. Even here, however, it has been pointed out by Marx and others that the satisfaction of one need (e.g., hunger) generates a number of other needs which, in turn, produce still other needs. Human needs tend to increase in relation to the increase of the complexity of a society. Since, for Sartre, a need is a negation, the dialectical structure of action (individual or collective) involves the overcoming of this negation by intervention in a practical field. But the interpretation of this basic need or negation as scarcity does not conform with certain facts. Thus, for example, there are primitive peoples who exist in scarcity but who do not have a 'history.'[25] Nor do they possess significant collective units charged with the task of overcoming this situation. In terms of Sartre's generalization this could not be possible. In addition, there are special cases in which extreme scarcity has led not to social action, but to inaction (e.g., in certain regions of India).

If we assume that revolutionary action would be paradigmatic of a dramatic response to scarcity, and if we further assume that Sartre's conception of the role of scarcity as a motivating factor in human history justifies the assertion that those who experience scarcity most painfully would react most violently to this condition (or 'negation'), then the historical facts of the English revolution of 1647, the Russian revolution, and the American revolution do not support Sartre's claims. For, in these revolutions those individuals most affected by scarcity were not the individuals whose *praxis* (in the broadest sense of the term) initiated these revolutions

---

motivational factor in human praxis and that this view is basic to Marxism. See: *The Sociology of Marx*, pp. 81-82.
24. CRD, p. 202.
25. Wilfrid Desan, *The Marxism of Jean-Paul Sartre*, p. 91.

or sustained them.[26] We may agree that need *(besoin)* or the subjective recognition of needs is at the basis of a great deal of social change; but it is not clear that the facticity of scarcity in itself necessarily brings about individual *praxis* or spontaneous collective unification. It is not necessarily the case that social conflict will result because there is not enough for everyone *(il n'y en pas assez pour tout)*[27] even though a self-conscious recognition of a need or 'lack' may indeed generate severe social conflicts. In the United States, for example, the Black-Americans who have been most active in protests, demonstrations, and rioting are not those who "do not have enough", but those who belong to the lower middle class (e.g., "blue-collar" workers), the middle class, and an educated minority. The Black-American is agitating for the satisfaction of social and psychological needs in most cases and not only basic economic needs. Extreme scarcity precludes effective social protest or effective social organization. The mere "absence of matter" *(pace* Sartre) does not necessarily cause the kind of *praxis* which would strive to overcome this concrete condition. *Rareté* or scarcity, then, is not the basic motivation for social *praxis,* group formation, or historical development nor is it such a basis in Marxist theory. In addition, the empirical evidence of history and dramatic social change indicates that Sartre's generalization is fundamentally false.

If we grant to Sartre that a subjective sense of 'need' is an essential stimulus to action, to group formation, we can see that conflict of some sort is inevitable since there is a direct struggle against the material world (insofar as the material conditions of life are inadequate to satisfy basic human needs) and, more significantly, a direct or indirect struggle against others. Thus, a great deal of social conflict is the result of an opposition between the subjective apprehension of needs on the part of one or more groups in a society. By virtue of need (understood in a material, social, and psychological sense) there is an inevitable totalization of material or practical entities and others (specifically other groups). Hence, human *praxis* conditions matter — its use, function, and value — and matter conditions *praxis.* When individuals act to satisfy their needs, their projects involve them in the material or practical milieu, a milieu which is 'humanized' and totalized. This relationship between man and the practical field reveals a dialectical circularity *(circularité dialectique)* and the individual is immersed in a reciprocal conditioning process or totalization in process. That is, the *praxis* of the individual synthesizes and unifies the phenomena in the social and practical milieu and he, in turn, is condi-

---

26. Crane Brinton, *The Anatomy of Revolution,* pp. 98-100.
27. *CRD,* p. 204.

tioned by the field of instrumentalities of which he is a part and in which he acts. The individual who acts in the social unity of instrumentalities "determines the zones, systems, privileged objects of this inert totality." There is a reciprocal interaction, then, between the material world (matter-in-itself) and the human world *(le monde de l'homme)*, the two modalities of being which constitute Sartrean 'reality.' The matter man acts upon is 'humanized matter' or *matière ouvrée*. The concrete relationship between man and a totalized material field provides the *material* basis for the totalization of men into specific groups. The *social* condition for the possibility of the emergence of groups is the recognition of the alterity of others. A more positive social factor is the recognition of a common interest, goal, or purpose.

For Sartre, the most primitive and immediate relationship between man and man is one of opposition or conflict. In *No Exit* Sartre had said that *L'enfer c'est l'autrui;* part of his *Critique* can be seen as an explication of that rhetorical assertion. In Sartre's thought, as in Hobbes', man is understood as the enemy of man; the *other,* Sartre avers, "carries in himself the menace of death."[28] Although such a pessimistic conception of human relations would seem to preclude social cooperation, Sartre maintains that the individual's experience of isolation and alienation reveals the impotence of his atomic existence. This social alienation is further aggravated by the worker's alienation from the products of his labor, the process by which, as Marx put it, the worker encounters the product of his labor as an alien objectification *(Vergegenständlichung)*, by which the tools and equipment he uses, the products he produces, become inert forces conditioning and circumscribing his existence.[29] The result or product of man's *praxis* now "acts upon" him, affecting his own concrete situation, ostensibly converting his life into an alienated existence. On this question of alienation there seems to be a basic opposition between Marx's position and that of Sartre. For Marx, the alienation of man can supposedly be overcome by means of the transformation of the capitalistic economic system, the destruction of class conflict, and the ultimate elimination of the State. For Sartre, however, human alienation cannot be transcended since

---

28. *Ibid.,* p. 208.
29. *Marx-Engels-Gesamtausgabe,* 1/3, p. 83. As Marx describes this process by which an individual is alienated from the product of his labor, he does so in language which seems to have been appropriated in Sartre's conception of the counterfinalities of human action. Thus, it is said that "This crystallization of social activity . . . this consolidation of what we ourselves produce into an objective power above us, growing out of our control, thwarting our expectations, bringing to naught our calculations, is one of the chief factors in histroical development." *The German Ideology,* pp. 22-24.

it is described as rooted in the *ontological* condition of man. Even assuming that the most ideal economic conditions existed or that complete social justice were attained in a utopian world, there could be no way in which the opposition and hostility Sartre ascribes to the relation between the individual and the other could be overcome since it is an essential ontological trait of the being of man. Sartre's phenomenological ontology of man precludes his acceptance of the quixotic social teleology (or eschatology) of Marxism. Rather, he must hold that alienation is an essential, pervasive characteristic of human existence. Even the suggestion which Sartre makes that *alienation* may be transcended if scarcity is eliminated from the world is unconvincing insofar as a residual threat of violence would seem to remain in terms of possible conflicts between classes or the recurrent appearance of what Sartre calls the "anti-man."

Social relations amongst men are characterized by the rebound of man's *praxs* upon itself through inorganic phenomena in a practical field. Although the immediate relation between man and the other is one of opposition, Sartre tends to agree with Georg Simmel that "relations of conflict do not by themselves produce a social structure, but only in cooperation with unifying forces."[30] The initial basis for this unification is *interest*. Interest arises when an individual is dependent upon a practical or material object for his subsistence or in order to satisfy a need or to realize a project. Interest is a particular relation of man to a thing in a social field.[31] A number of individuals waiting for an airplane at an airport may be relatively indifferent to one another. But, if the plane is late, there is a gradual increase of concern, a subtle unifying factor. A common concern or interest brings about totalizing activity on the part of the members of this loosely structured 'group' *(serialité)*. Whether the commonly shared goal is ambiguous or clearly defined, it provides an intentional object for concern. This underlying teleological factor characterizing groups-information is described as *finality*. Every finality, in the dialectic of experience, brings about a reaction, a counterfinality. Thus, for example, a worker may join a union in order to protect his own rights and the rights of his fellow workers. But it may happen that the union officials attain more power than is desirable and may ultimately become oppressive in regard to

---

30. Georg Simmel, *Conflict* and *The Web of Group-Affiliations*, p. 20.
31. *CRD*, p. 261. Although interest in a material object in a practical field may be the basis for many social unifications, spiritual finalities have played (and continue to play) a significant role in social unification. This is accounted for by Sartre in terms of a commonly shared "idea." His analyses of the social function of such ideas are, however, rather incomplete in light of the various descriptions of the role of values and ideals in social cohesion which can be found in standard American sociological theories.

the interest of the workers. Human action in terms of a given finality runs the risk of generating an undesirable counterfinality. This paradoxical aspect of social relations illustrates the complex dialectical process of social relations. The free *praxis* of individuals transforms the material or practical field; this change, in turn, affects the social relations of individuals. These dual totalities, then, condition the individual affected by them: that is, the freedom of the individual brings about a necessity which 'limits' that freedom. Although the initiation of *praxis* is a free project, the dialectical processes brought about by this action are not merely causally determined, but necessitated. Although Sartre intends to preserve individual liberty in social action, he admits a host of conditioning factors which curtail, if not negate, this freedom. This is even more obviously the case in his description of the structure of the unified group.

The primitive basis of group formation, the seriality, is a mere juxtaposition of individuals or a loosely associated serial relationship among individuals. A seriality is a passive, inert structure in which each person is basically alone, existing in a random multiplicity. In this diffuse social structure the individual as such is impotent (i.e., it is a *liaison d'impuissance*). The individual experiences himself as other than the other members of the seriality and exists, in relation to the others, in a reciprocity of antagonism *(un sérialité est . . . une première structure d'altérité, fondée sur la réciprocité d'antagonisme).*[32] The link between each individual and every other in a seriality is unstable, a social structure which tends towards dissolution. To return to an earlier illustration, we can say that the individuals awaiting the arrival of an airplane at an airport form a seriality. A common concern unifies them in a transitory social relationship. But as soon as the plane arrives and the individuals board the plane, there is a dissolution of the temporary unity (even though the group may be totalized by another as, say, "the passengers of flight 501"). A seriality, then, is a 'negative,' transitory social structure which lacks the cohesive influence of a pervasive common threat, common danger, common object, or common idea. Despite its inadequacy, the seriality provides the social conditions for the possibility of group formation.

Although a seriality tends towards disintegration, it can be the basis of a cohesive social unity if each individual becomes aware of the potentiality

---

32. *Ibid.*, p. 354. In some of his amplified discussions of serialities he seems to depart from this description insofar as he speaks of serialities as diffused social structures characterized either by a kind of passive indifference amongst individuals or an atomization of individuals. In the sense that one may be a member of a seriality without being conscious of it, it does not seem to be necessary that relationships of antagonism be manifested at all.

implicit in the seriality and is willing to act in such a way as to bring about a more stable social unity. Thus, for example, a *rassemblement* of individuals living in the same community who desire to prevent the building of a bridge in their locale are brought together by virtue of a common interest. But if they remain a seriality, they will be ineffective. In a sense, there is a contradiction between the individual as a member of the passive seriality and the individual as dialectical mediator — an individual who imposes unity on the seriality (i.e., totalizes it). This contradiction can be overcome either through withdrawal from the seriality or, in a positive sense, by a concerted action directed by a recognition of a common threat. The indistinct relationship between individuals comprising a seriality creates an ambiguous social relationship. Serialities tend to resemble inorganic entities, passive phenomena incapable of action. In the above illustration, the members of the community may feel that they are being victimized by the organzation building the bridge, but they may be unable to act together in order to oppose this threat. The members of this "escaping unity" *(unité fuyante)* experience a vague powerlessness, a psychological sense of disunity (despite their physical justaposition and common concern). Each member of a seriality is basically suspicious or hostile toward the other. Each individual experiences the "lack" or need he shares with others and he recognizes the finality to be sought, but the tendency of the seriality toward inertia prevents him from seeing what is necessary to accomplish that finality. The individual sees himself as isolated within a tenuous unity, lacking a significant synthetic objective, lacking a sense of cooperative concern with a dominant 'idea.' Despite its weakness as a social instrument of action, Sartre claims that the seriality is anterior to group formations and is the primitive social structure out of which groups emerge.

If there is an initiation of direct action, if some concrete commitment takes place within a seriality, then contagious reactions appear and the social process generates the proto-group. This emergent process transforms an inert social structure into a group-in-fusion *(groupe en fusion)*. The synthetic object which unifies the group is the result of the free *praxis* of individuals, the "epicenters" of individual choice and resolution by which the rudiments of a unified group are formed. The group is a common *praxis* which results from a multiplicity of free choices by which individuals commit themselves to a social unity which demands a degree of self-sacrifice. The recognition of a common danger of threat leads to the fusion of groups, the emergence of collective *praxis*. The essence of human *praxis* is *dépassement*, surpassing or transcending the existing situation.[33] How-

---

33. Mary Warnock, *The Philosophy of Sartre*, p. 147. Cp. *CRD*, p. 99. The terminology Sar-

ever, it is to be noted that the term *dépassement* is used in the sense of Hegel's notion of *aufhebung,* the surpassing *and* preserving of the fundamental structures already present in a new synthesis. In the *Critique* Sartre explicitly remarks that the dialectical movement in social processes permits the comprehension of the goals of human activity which simply represent *le dépassement et le maintien du donné dans un acte qui va du présent vers l'avenir.*

The group-in-fusion is further unified when another social unit totalizes it. Thus, for example, the mine owners in Pennsylvania at the turn of the century totalize the *group en fusion* (the mine workers) and thereby generate a greater sense of group identity. The opposition by the other group provides the members of the group-in-fusion with a unifying synthetic objective, albeit an antagonistic one. The individual members of the seriality now adopt the perspective of what Sartre calls the third man *(le tiers),* that is, an individual who recognizes himself as one with the other members of the seriality which had previously been experienced as alien. The member of the emerging group, through the recognition of the totalizing activity of the non-group (or other group), now realizes a common danger, a synthetic objective. Hence, the individual, as mediator, totalizes his own loosely structured group and, hence, solidifies the unity of his group.[34] The members of the group are, then, unified by a common *praxis* and a common need *(exigence commune).*

Ostensibly, the transition to group formation is not characterized by necessity or mechanistic determinism. Whether this is actually the case, in Sartre's account of group solidification, is a question we must deal with below. At any rate, the various stages of development of social organization are dependent upon the presence and activity of individuals. The dynamic, renewed participation of individuals in social evolution makes this process a matter of decision and choice. This development is intelligi-

---

tre uses to describe the process of "surpassing" a present limiting condition had been used by Henri Lefebvre to describe the dialectical process in the Hegelian phenomenology. Thus, he wrote that "Négation dialectique — négation de la négation — implique *dépassement* effectif, créateur de figures nouvelles de la conscience . . . ce mouvement qui depasse a chaque moment 'existant' implique une *histoire,* une explication, une dialectique." *L'Existentialisme,* Paris, 1946, p. 197.

34. *CRD.* p 398. The only substantive change in Sartre's hypothetical concept of 'the third man' from *Being and Nothingness* to the *Critique* is that he is no longer restricted to the factory model he used in the earlier work in which the third man is the factory owner who "totalizes" his workers and thereby converts *them* into a group. In the *Critique* there emerges a notion of the third man mediator who is immanent in a group and who has a central function in group solidification.

ble or 'rational' insofar as the intentions of those comprising a group-information presuppose a consciousness of this teleological process. In addition, the process in intelligible in the sense that Sartre seems to believe there is no unknowable or inaccessible process occurring which cannot be examined in the light of a critical dialectic. It is for this reason, as we shall see, that he tends to undermine or to deny the role of the irrational in social processes. Man is conditioned by some social facts over which he seems to have no control, but he is a conditioning agent who can, to some extent, shape the direction of social movements. There is a reciprocal interrelationship of the practical field, the individual and the group to which he belongs, the group and other groups, and the groups and the practical fields in which they manifest their action. The particular relationship between the individual and the group is ostensibly a contingent one. What is supposedly true of the individual's relationship to the group is also true, *mutatis mutandis,* of the being of the group as such. This contingency, however, seems more obvious in the initial stages of group formation than in the conditions characterizing the fully established group. The basis of social development, of social power, seems to shift from individuals to the group in itself as the social unit which becomes more cohesive, more determinate in structure.

The self-conscious recognition on the part of the individual member of a group of the common purpose of the group leads him to synthesize the group as a totality. There is the emergence of a unifying inner orientation within the group which Sartre (unlike Lewin and Moreno) thinks is intelligible. The group is now a constituted dialectic (*dialectique constituée),* the resultant of the free *praxis* of individuals engaged in intentional acts. The objective structure of a group is primarily determined by the classification or description of the group by an individual observer (or group of observers) outside the group. There is, then, a dual constituting of the group as totality, both from within and without. The members of the group determine its unity through shared purposes, aims, or values. Those who do not share this inner orientation objectify the group as a totality (an alien totality) and constitute its structure and nature from their perspective. Often, the observer or observers of a group posits the group as an integral totality and thereby "sees" the group as, or interprets the group as, more unified in spirit than it is in fact. If this understanding of the group becomes known by its members, it then contributes to its further unification.

When a member of a group is dependent upon that group, or appeals to its power or relies upon its protection, he trusts in it and depends upon the "praxis under oath" *(praxis jurée).*[35] For, it is this which determines the proper function of the group. This relationship of dependency is characterized by a conception of the group as a determinate (though dialectically complex) social structure, a conception which is primarily derived from the recognition of the group by others. For the member of the group the group is an *objet practique;*[36] but for those who totalize it from without it is an antagonistic social force. Sartre insists that the inner synthesis of groups rests upon a response to the externally imposed totalization of those outside the group. In this regard, he seems to be providing a sociological application of Hegel's notion that "Self-consciousness *(Selbstbewusstsein)* attains its satisfaction in another self-consciousness."[37] That is, the recognition of my group by others and the subsequent sense of antagonism generates a heightened self-consciousness on my part of my membership in a group and my concern with its being. The group becomes, then, a unified multiplicity *(multiplicité unifiée)* capable of organized practice *(praxis organisée).* The individual truly becomes a member of a group by virtue of a dual process: the subjective interiorization of the multiplicity *(intériorisant la multiplicité)* and the realization that the group to which one belongs is totalized by those outside the group. There is a dialectical interrelationship among these social processes.

By virtue of mediated reciprocity *(reciprocité medieé)* the individual qua member of the group benefits, in his own activity, from the activity of others. The group becomes the communal structure of the individual's actions. The function of the individual within the group is both a task which must be performed and a relation between each individual and all the members of the group. When an individual has a specific task to perform this gives him a determinate place in a group and establishes reciprocal interactions between the individual and the group which have the function of creating a more cohesive social unit. As a member of a group, the individual's action emerges in relation to a common power *(commun pouvoir)* directed towards a common objective *(objectif commun).* Although the actualization of the power of the group is possible because of

---

35. *Ibid.,* p. 556.
36. *Ibid.*
37. G. W. F. Hegel, *Phänomenologie des Geistes,* in *Sämmtliche Werke,* Hamburg, 1907, p. 121. The dialectical relationship between a given group and another is clearly modeled upon Hegel's conception of the relationship between a self and the other in his phenomenology. The significant difference is that Sartre sometimes suggests that if scarcity is eliminated, then the relationships amongst groups may be cooperative. However, the ultimate alterity in the human world which Sartre now describes as the "anti-man" seems to be a recurring phenomenon in history.

the free practice of individuals, their practice is itself determined "as an ephemeral mediation between the common power and the common objective."[38] Individual practice is a "mediation" because it supresses itself in order to serve a common end *(fin commune)*, to achieve a shared finality. The power of the individual within a group is expressed in a concrete function and is, for each member of the group, "the right to fulfil his particular task."[39]

Although the free practice of the individual is the ostensible basis upon which group action is founded, there is a certain inevitable tension between the individual's *praxis* and the organized practice of the group. It is for this reason that Sartre holds that "the only specific and direct action of an organized group is . . . its organization and reorganization . . . its action upon its members."[40] The group, as it were, must protect itself against the tendency of the individual's practice to project itself beyond the common end of the group as such. Sartre, like Simmel, is aware of the "positive and integrating role of antagonism," and he is also aware that conflict can be such an integrating factor insofar as "a certain amount of discord, inner divergence and outer controversy, is . . . tied up with the very elements that ultimately hold the group together."[41] The structure of the group entails, for Sartre as well as Simmel, contradictory tensions *(tensions contradictoires)*. For Sartre, however, these 'internal tensions' could easily bring about the dissolution of the group if there is no coercive power or force to enforce the cooperative action of individual members of the group. In this sense, the group must have some power by which to limit the freedom of the individuals who have, by virtue of their free *praxis*, contributed to the existence of the group. Implicitly, the individual has transferred his powers and rights to the group and has renounced a great deal of his freedom.

One of the ways in which some of the internal tensions of groups is overcome is (and here I am presenting an interpolation of Sartre's account of the matter) by means of the indirect coercive power of a dominant "idea." Although the group's cognitive orientation is primarily related to action, the unity of the group is also sustained by virtue of an implicit

---

38. *CRE*, p. 470.
39. *Ibid.*, p. 463.
40. *Ibid.*, p. 474. What this seems to mean, in Sartre's terms, is that the group is sustained by the constituting totalization of individuals within the group (as well as that of other groups) and that members of the group are subject to the constituting totalization of the group itself. This dialectical process would seem to entail a persistent tension in a group between each individual and the group itself.
41. Georg Simmel, *op. cit.*, pp. 17-18.

understanding of the 'idea' which the group imposes on itself and which is assimilated by the members of the group. The dominant idea adopted by a group functions as an interior norm *(norme intérieure)*,[42] a unifying conception which creates a common bond among members of a group, an implicit self-understanding which cannot be shared by those outside the group. Although Sartre does not refer to it directly, we may interpret what he means in this regard in terms of the *ethos* of a group, the shared meanings, attitudes, beliefs, and approved ways of behaving which characterize closely knit group formations. At any rate, the mutually accepted 'idea' functions as a centripetal social force which produces, as Simmel had argued, "the consensus and concord of interacting individuals, as against their discords, separations, and disharmonies."[43] Common convictions, implicitly accepted by all, provide for cohesive groups and are often symbolically reinforced by ritual, initiation, ceremony, or the expression of fidelity by means of an oath. These overt performative actions do not *per se* reveal the *ethos* which joins together members of a group since, as is often the case, the group's self-conception and primary intentions are not apparent to the detached observer. Although Sartre's conception of the group's dominant idea is not identical with the *ethos* of a group, it seems to serve the same purpose.

The Coercive Power of the Group

Although the group, in Sartre's phenomenological portrait, comes into being out of the free *praxis* of a number of individuals, there is a counter-dialectical (or anti-dialectic) tendency toward inertia. Groups tend towards increasing rigidity and tend to become what we might call static totalities. There is a tendency to stifle dissent, to undermine the vitalizing power of internal tensions and antagonisms. This tendency is closely linked with the necessary conversion of the individual into the common individual *(l'individu commun)* whose existence in a group is made coercive by means of what Sartre refers to, in somewhat dramatic terms, as *terreur* or terror. *Terreur* has the function of preventing the group from lapsing into an ineffective seriality. It not only includes threats of physical retaliation on the part of the group, but any form of coercion which has the function of preventing the dissolution of the group.

In order to preserve the group from disintegration, the group itself places severe restrictions upon its members. The internal danger to the

---

42. *CRD* , p. 502. This notion of the development of an interior norm in groups is explicitly described by Simmel in his analysis of group affiliation.
43. Georg Simmel, *loc. cit.*

group is countered by the demand for allegiance to the social unit in the form of the oath. The oath binds the individual to the group and establishes the condition for the use of coercion against the individual. *Terreur* involves the threat of expulsion from the group, ostracism, or physical punishment. The oath and terror are intimately related since the oath is an affirmation of violence *(affirmation de la violence)*. The common oath commits the individual to an agreement that he shall suffer some penalty if his actions threaten the dissolution of the group. The individual's being-in-the-group *(être-dans-le-groupe)* is a free consent to accept the right of the group to his *praxis* and the absolute right of all over each individual *(droit absolu de tous sur chacun.)*[44] Through the oath the group gives itself an ontological status which diminishes the danger of excessive differentiation and provides for the sanction of the oath, the coercive power of "terror." By means of the oath each individual has limited his freedom through the other, has granted to the others the right of violence over him. The common limit of the individual's freedom is characterized by Sartre as the fraternity of terror *(la fraternité . . . de le Terreur)*.[45] This is necessary, it is argued, because the oath without the threat of penalty would be impotent.

Sartre seems to stress the necessity of the coercive power of the group *(le caractére coercitif du groupe)* basically because he had, in *L'Être et le néant,* said that the essence of human reality is freedom and that being-for-others is a relationship of conflict, frustration, hostility, and mutual negation. He has always emphasized the "alienating reality of the other." Given this philosophical anthropology, it is not surprising to see Sartre reverting to Hobbes' notion that "covenants without the sword are but words, and of no strength to secure a man at all." The individual, in order to benefit from the common freedom granted by means of group membership, must submit his free *praxis* to the sovereignty of the group itself. One must be sceptical when Sartre assures us that the interiorization of this common freedom is "the real power of his individual freedom."[46] Rather, it would seem that the individual has transferred his freedom to the group as such. It is paradoxical that even though the group is ostensibly formed to achieve a common end, to transcend the relative impotence of the individual, to satisfy the needs of the individual, is ostensibly an instrument for the individual's use, that the individual is entirely subject to the interoconditioning of the group, is subservient to its power. The maturation of a

---

44. *CRD*, pp. 449-450.
45. *Ibid.*, p. 456.
46. *Ibid.*, p. 491.

group entails the negation of individual freedom in any true sense of the word. Since the essence of man, as Sartre conceives of it, conflicts with his social role as member of a group, we must assume that, for Sartre, there will be a perpetual tension between the individual and the group. In addition, we can understand why he insists upon the coercive power of the group insofar as coercion seems the only means of unifying individuals who, as Sartre has described them, are basically incapable of spontaneous cooperation. In this respect, Sartre's ontology of man determines his conception of the structure of groups in much the same way as Hobbes' psychology of man determined his conception of civil society and its sovereignty. Sartre's general view seems to be that as long as *rareté* or scarcity exists in the world there will be conflict between groups or classes. In addition, he also shares the Marxian view (especially that of Lenin) that the importance of a common end justifies the sacrifice of the individual, the conversion of the individual into an instrument of a collectivity. The underlying, unstated model for Sartre's phenomenology of groups is a collectivistic, political social unity. What is ironical about his subordination of the individual to the group (or class) is that it has recently been challenged by revisionists like Leszek Kolakowski who attacks the "historiosophical vision" which assumes that the individual is totally subordinate to, and negated by, the "messianic hope" which becomes the only law of life and which demands complete sacrifice of the individual in order to bring about the "new era."[47]

Kolakowski, obviously under the influence of the existentialists, emphasizes the responsibility of each individual for his actions and denies that a historical destiny or philosophy of history absolves the individual. It is ironical to see Kolakowski, a Marxist revisionist, moving in the direction of the early Sartre and to see Sartre, ostensibly a revisionist as well, moving closer to the very view which Kolakowski is attacking under his influence. Although there is little doubt that, in the domain of social action, Sartre clearly describes the individual as subservient to the interests of the group, it is unfair to suggest that he is advocating a kind of totalitarianism.[48] However, the absorption of the individual by the group is presented as an ineluctable process if the group is to become an effective social unity. It is difficult to believe that the group which Sartre describes could be one in which the individual is able to manipulate the group in the interest of his

---

47. Leszek Kolakowski, "Responsibility and History," in *Existentialism versus Marxism*, pp. 291-292.
48. Mary Warnock, *op. cit.*, p. 175.

own security.⁴⁹ His description of the *groupe en contrainte* as a social organization in which there is a materialization of terror *(une matérialisation de la Terreur)* in the form of instruments of restraint makes us sceptical concerning his sanguine remarks about the preservation of individual liberty within such a group. Strictly speaking, the individual, as a member of a group, has no natural rights at all. As such, the individual is reduced to his function since, in organized activity, *la fonction est une définition positive de l'individu commun.*"⁵⁰ A man defined by his function, treated as a common individual, is surely an object (not, as Sartre would have us believe, a subject), an instrument which must serve the interest of the sovereign group. As a member of the typical group Sartre describes, the individual is more alienated from his human nature than he is in the capitalistic societies Sartre criticizes. In Sartre's language each individual is the alien "other" for the group and the group is the alien "other" for each member of it. The sovereignty of the group seems to entail the negation of individual freedom. The individual's *praxis* is entirely subject to the coercive power of the group.

Necessity and the Neglect of the Irrational

The most valuable contribution which Sartre has made to an understanding of group-formation or social organization has been the heuristic method of dialectical reasoning as an instrument for the interpretation of social phenomena. In agreement with Hegel, Sartre maintains that history in general and social development in particular (the latter as we've pointed out, is fused with the former) manifests a dialectical process. He disagrees with Hegel, however, by denying "that all dialectic movement culminates in an absolute which lies beyond individual consciousness."⁵¹ For Sartre, man acts upon the world through a "living dialectic," by means of his intentional projects. In his *Critique* he is in general agreement, as we

---

49. *CRD*, p. 498.
50. *Ibid.*, p. 463.
51. Arthur Lessing, "Marxist Existentialism," *Review of Metaphysics*, XX (1967), p. 473. It may be said that there is a suggestion in the *Critique* that the ultimate totalization in which individuals, directly or indirectly, participate is history itself. In this regard, if there is an absolute in Sartre's later thought it is history itself. It is certainly plausible to argue that the postulated "humanistic Us" of *Being and Nothingness* which was said to be possible only on the basis of the existence of a transcendent "third" (or God) is, in the *Critique*, now clearly a realistic goal to be attained in and through history. That man can transform himself and recover the "human totality" is certainly a sentiment which is often expressed in Marxist literature.

have said, with Marx's remark in *The Eighteenth Brumaire of Louis Napoleon* that "men make their own history, but . . . they do not make it under circumstances chosen by themselves, but under circumstances directly encountered . . . transmitted from the past." The only concrete universal (in Hegel's terms) for Sartre is *l'homme historique*, a being immersed in temporality and finitude. The dialectic is not an abstract notion, not only a kind of thinking or reasoning (e.g., as it appears to be in Plato's discussion of "dialectical reasoning" in *The Republic*). Rather, it is "the very structure of concrete reality itself."[52] Dialectical reasoning is presumably an asymptotic approximation to an actual immanent dialectical process. The complex, qualitative changes which characterize sociotemporal succession do seem to manifest something like a dialectical process. To be sure, the method of dialectical reasoning is only one way in which social phenomena can be interpreted or understood. The reciprocal interrelationship of individuals in social processes may or may not, *in concreto*, be structured dialectically. This is a question concerning how phenomena are to be interpreted. But the basic question is, what method of describing or explaining social phenomena has the most viable heuristic value? Sartre's dialectical interpretation of social developments (which seems to be a synthesis of Hegelian, Marxist and sociological conceptions of dialectic) is, with some modifications, a useful, valuable method for the interpretation of social phenomena. However, certain aspects of his application of dialectics to social relations and social developments are theoretically questionable.

Although it is true that Sartre's dialectic is a conception of a "spontaneous will pitted against the inert resistance of the material world,"[53] it is more than this since it also includes the way in which human actions rebound against man's intentions. Counterfinalities are also part of the dialectical process of social existence. Sartre refers to inert forces (the practico-inert) or socio-material factors which limit human freedom in terms of the inertia which plagues social processes as well. Groups are subject to a reversion to the inert serialities from which they have emerged as well as the rigidity and ossification which infects powerful social organizations. Although Sartre refers to an anti-dialectic in these cases, there is a tension in his own position since *all* social processes are described as if they were dialectical. In *What is literature?* he had described the anti-dialectic which wears away dialectical processes as itself a form of dialectic. Insofar as the anti-dialectic acts upon man's projects in a social milieu it has an ef-

---

52. A Kojève, "Hegel, Marx et le Christianisme," *Critique I*, (1949), p. 339.
53 G. Lichtheim, *Marxism in Modern France*, p. 98.

ficacy in a dialectic *en cours*. A counterfinality or a practico-inert phenomenon acts upon man as a dialectical force which conflicts with his own projects, with his original intentions. At times, Sartre seems aware that the conception of an anti-dialectic is misleading;[54] but, on the other hand, he often seems to refer to it as a non-dialectical countervailing force. But insofar as any phenomenon (e.g., in Sartre's illustration, the floods which ultimately resulted from a deforestation program in China) is the result of man's action upon natural phenomena or upon social behavior in general, it must be considered as a *positive* dialectical process and not a negative anti-dialectic.

In regard to the conception of dialectic in general, Sartre claims that he is sympathetic to Kierkegaard's emphasis upon the primacy of concrete actuality in relation to thought, upon the brute realities which can neither be surpassed nor changed by knowledge,[55] and the nature of the "adventure" of the single individual. But he seems to undermine the central characteristic of Kierkegaard's "dialectic of life," the notion that individual existence is characterized by contingency and not necessity. Under the influence of Hegel, Sartre seems to deny the contingency of human existence, to admit, at least in regard to social organization, necessity in human existence. It has been charged that he has completely denied the existentialist contingency,[56] that he has described the individual's existence

---

54. "*Qu'est-ce que* literature?" *Situations, II*, (1948), p. 86. In this essay he had said that the "anti-dialectic" is itself dialectical. Although Marx himself does refer to the way in which human labor can rebound upon individuals and circumscribe them by alien powers or forces, he does not describe this negating process whereby life processes produce results that undermine those processes as "anti-dialectical" insofar as such a "counterfinality" is itself the product of intelligible dialectical movements. The primary erosive force which Marx identified in history was the alienation of man from the product of his social energy — this was *the* counterfinality in human history. As Adam Schaff has described this notion in Marx's thought, "there unfolds a process in the course of which, through the objectification and reification of human activity and under certain conditions, the creations of men become independent of their creators, and then fully autonomous in their functioning; and so, they subordinate man to things, and lead to the phenomenon of *alienation.*" [*Marxism and the Human Individual*, p. 105]. This form of social existence is not the result of a social practico-inert, but is a positive power which presumably undermines man's freedom. It is the result of a historical process of development. While Sartre's notion of anti-dialectical forces is an interesting amplification of Marx's general observation, it is not a Marxist notion in any sense.
55. *CRD*, pp. 19-20.
56. Mary Warnock, *op. cit.*, p. 180. Although I am basically sympathetic to this interpretation of Sartre's later work, it is not so much that he deliberately abandons the perspective of the contingent individual as that there is a real tension in his social thought

in a group in terms of necessity. This is implied in his assertion that the structures of the "functional organization" *(organisation fonctionnelle)*, insofar as their material, inorganic form has been "freely" interiorized by the group, are characterized by the "necessity of liberty"[57] — the liberty of the group, not the individual. Through membership in a group each individual is affected by the inertia of the gorup and is converted into an inorganic being *(être inorganique)*. Ineluctably, the individual is incorporated into, or appropriated by, the group. The common individual as inorganic being "surrounds," "limits," and conditions my action, but it is ostensibly the foundation of my *praxis*.[58] Surely, if the common individual is affected by the inertia of the group and is converted into an inorganic being *(être inorganique)*. Ineluctably, the individual is in-praxis, we can no longer speak of free practice at all.

One of the unfortunate diachronic or durational aspects of group organization is the tendency towards inflexibility, immobility and ossification. In bureaucratic organizations the very rigidity of the social structure prevents the individuals functioning within it from attaining desirable goals or ends. In this sense, it may be said that the success of certain social organizations contains the seeds of their failure to satisfy the aims or needs which the group was ostensibly created to serve. Once such a process of ossification occurs, the innovator, the creative individual is seen as "other, stranger, suspect."[59] What undermines Sartre's conception of the structure of groups is his apparent willingness to ascribe these tendencies towards inertia as necessary and inevitable. The ultimate counterfinality of group organization is the gradual deprivation of individual freedom. To speak of a paradoxical "necessity of liberty" does not mitigate the necessitarian structure of the dialectic of group solidification. Although man's freedom emerges in "situation," group membership is a situation of facticity in which this freedom is no longer possible. Because of the prominance given to groups in Sartre's social phenomenology, we may assume that it is not,

---

between his desire to retain the existentialist conception of the human condition and to promote a form of social organization that will eliminate social injustice, scarcity and the negativities of the world as it is. In his explication of the process of group formation he begins to grant less and less significance to the individual and to grant coercive power to the group insofar as its finality is commensurate with a revised Marxist goal. There is no doubt that even the individualism Sartre has done so much to conserve and preserve would have to be sacrificed in the social world he seems to prescribe for man insofar as organized practice transcends the value of the contingently existing individual.

57. *CRD*, p. 494.
58. *Ibid.*
59. *Ibid.*, p. 625.

as he says, individual *praxis* which is the motivating factor in social development and history; rather, it is coercive social collectivities. The social dialectic which is described in the *Critique* deprives man of as much freedom as does the dialectical materialism of the dogmatic Marxists who are criticized for ignoring the value and freedom of the individual. Freedom as a dialectically expressed negation of the negations which threaten the realization of human potentialities is clearly curtailed in the social structures Sartre describes, especially when he empowers the group with the constraining instrument of the threat of violence. The individual within a group possesses only a common power and no individual power. Individual alienation and powerlessness are exchanged for the sovereign power of the group and a common freedom *(la liberté commune)* is substituted for individual freedom. But this common freedom belongs to all and none.

Although Sartre intended to preserve the freedom of the individual, to avoid the "inhuman anthropology" of the contemporary Marxists, to conserve human freedom in the face of the surrounding totalities which limit this freedom, he introduces necessity into his account of the dialectic of social relations to such an extent that he has, *malgré lui*, undermined his intention. He describes dialectical processes as inevitable, proceeding from stage to stage in accordance with a necessity implicit in all social phenomena. Every finality, for example, must generate a counterfinality. The dialectical process itself generates a necessary countervailing social force (the anti-dialectic). The free individual in a group inevitably is converted into the common individual and the common individual is ineluctably transformed into an inorganic being, a totality which the group uses for its own ends. The individual must totalize the phenomena he encounters. Scarcity dominates all *praxis*. The coercive threat of *terreur* is necessary in order to retain social cohesion. Sartre's social analysis is shot through with the unveiling of necessity. Clearly, once an individual takes an oath (symbolically or actually), once he is committed to a group, he is caught in the complex web of dialectical necessity.

Sartre undermines his intention in the *Critique* primarily because of the implicit influence of Hegel on his interpretation of social phenomena. Just as Hegel thought that historical events are dominated by an overriding "destiny," so, too, does Sartre refer to the 'destiny' of social developments. Just as Hegel had assumed that all reality is entirely intelligible, so, too, does Sartre seem to hold that all social phenomena are intelligible. Hegel, in his *Vorlesungen über die Philosophie der Geschichte,* had been concerned with the rational in history and, hence, was uninterested in the apparently contingent except insofar as it could be understood in terms of a dialectical necessity governing human history. As has recently been said, Hegel ignored the "irrational, and the merely contingent of which world history largely consists."[60] History is universal history *(Weltgeschichte)*, the true subject of which is the universal, not the individual.[61] The particular aim of individuals is an expression of a universal principle which is manifested in a rational, necessary process of development. The individual's relation to history in Hegel's philosophy of history is parallel to the relationship between the individual and the group in Sartre's sociology. The individual's *praxis* contributes to the growth of social groups which have a power and significance which transcends that of the individual. The freedom of the individual in Sartre's work is sacrificed for the freedom of "humanity" just as the individual is sacrificed, for Hegel, in order that the "Idea" of freedom be realized in time. Sartre writes in the Hegelian mode when he asserts that "critical experience" (understood in terms of a rational dialectic) is nothing else but the "fundamental identity of a singular life and human history" *(l'identite' fondamentale d'une vie singulière et de l'histoire humaine)*.

It is maintained that necessity, as the apodictic structure of dialectical experience, results from the necessary process of interiorizing the exterior and exteriorizing the interior.[62] In the process of interiorizing an external phenomenon human action is affected by necessity. Sartre's commitment to a dialectical model forces him to postulate opposing forces in his analysis of social processes. Since he is already assuming that dialectical reason is the only access to social phenomena, that social phenomena are translucently intelligible, he is led to embrace an apriorist, necessitarian ontology of social processes. It is his hyper-rationalism which leads Sartre to introduce into his sociology a description of what seem to be logically necessary relationships. Inadvertently, he proceeds from a social phenomenology to a prescriptive, rationalistic account of how social processes ought to occur. However, the most obvious chink in the armor of Sartre's analysis of group formations is his neglect of the irrational factors influencing the nature and form of social processes. This neglect can be

---

60. Louis Dupré, *The Philosophical Foundations of Marxism*, p. 64.
61. -Herbert Marcuse, *Reason and Revolution*, p. 229.
62. *CRD*, p. 157. It is to be noted that there is no question here, as there had been in *Being and Nothingness*, of "choosing" this facticity of social existence. Throughout the *Critique* there is the implicit notion that the factual situation in which an individual finds himself is one which is, for the most part, already constituted. The concrete facticity in which man finds himself is by no means a matter of a free "choice." The implicit treatment of the facticity of man in the world of social existence in the *Critique* is far more convincing that Sartre's account of it in *Being and Nothingness*.

emphasized by indicating how Le Bon and Freud have dealt with the "psychological group."

Although some of the conceptual models used by Le Bon are outmoded or, at least, are metempirical (e.g., the ostensible influence of a "racial unconsciousness"), and although his study is primarily concerned with "crowds," his understanding of the irrational factors contributing to group formation is applicable to the social phenomena which Sartre has analyzed. Despite his earlier psychological insights, Sartre has practically neglected the influence of emotions and sentiments (what Pareto described as *residues*) upon the process of group formation in his *Critique*. He is at pains to deny one of the basic assumptions of Le Bon (and Durkheim as well) — that individuals comprising a group contribute to the development of a "collective mind." For, Sartre denies that the group "temporalizes" itself as *une Gestalt ou un organisme ou une hyperconscience*. He desires to avoid all mystical or magical interpretations of the nature of groups.[63] Although alluding to a theory such as Durkheim's, what he says applies to Le Bon as well and, to some extent, to Gurvitch. Nevertheless, a group is described as fundamentally a synthetic unity which is unified by the organized activities of individuals under the aegis of an oath and the threat of expulsion or physical punishment. The group-information is primarily an intentional social construct, a social unit formed in terms of rational, self-conscious ends or commonly shared 'ideas.'

The origination of social units lies in a gradual emergence of an interest focused upon a material or practical object. And the overall, underlying cause of social action is a socio-economic factor, scarcity. In such cases, it is clear that the need *(besoin)* or negation which is to be overcome is rational in terms of the reality situation individuals find themselves in. There is a sense, however, in which Sartre held that the group transcends the individuals comprising it insofar as it possesses greater power, authority, and sovereignty than any of its members. There may not be, in his account of groups, a collective consciousness as such, but it is clear that the "common individual" may be said to possess, as a member of a group, a common consciousness *(conscience commune)*. However, Sartre is consistent in denying that the group is a hyperorganic entity which is beyond the experience of the individual.[65] In this regard one is inclined to sympathize

---

63. *Ibid.*, p. 507.
64. Cf. Emile Durkheim, *De la Division du Travail*, Paris, 1902.
65. *CRD*, p. 509. In this regard, it may be said that Sartre desired to give an empirical, if dialectical, account of the being of groups which would obviate any notion of an organic or organismic social totality.

with his quasi-naturalistic conception of group structure. On the other hand, the non-logical factors contributing to group formation which are pointed out by Le Bon are correctives to Sartre's assumption of a purely rational basis for the genesis of group formation and action. Le Bon maintained that unconscious phenomena play a dominant part in the actions of individuals forming a group. The individual who becomes a member of a group acquires "a sentiment of invincible power" which he would not have if he remained isolated. In addition, it is said that in a group every sentiment and act is "contagious" to such an extent that the individual would sacrifice his own personal interests for the sake of the collective interest.[66] Although Sartre refers, in passing, to such contagious reactions, he tends to minimize their importance as unifying factors in group solidification because he believes that consciously recognized ends are more influential in leading the individual to become part of a group. The ambiguity of spontaneous group formations is obscured in his account of group formation. We can see this in a concrete illustration he uses, one which parallels those of LeBon: that is, the "storming of the Bastille" in 1789. Sartre claims that this event indicates the way in which a common danger and a common object can convert a seriality (in this instance, the *quartier St.-Antoine*) into an organized group. This is an unfortunate illustration since the attack upon the Bastille was motivated by fear of the intervention of foreign regiments which, it was thought, would surround the city. (Sartre, incidentally, neglects to mention the role which this *rumor* had on the behavior of individuals on this occasion.)

The ostensible purpose of the attack — to withdraw the arms stored there — was undermined because the governor (de Launay) had already agreed to allow the equipment to be withdrawn. The attack on the Bastille was the result of the irrational action of two men (who were ignorant of the previously made agreement) who invaded the inner courts and drew the fire of the governor's garrison. The "Storming of the Bastille" was the result of a chaotic series of events resulting in mutual misunderstanding (on the part of the governor, his garrison, and the group gathered outside the Bastille).[67] One may say that a dialectic was at work here; but it was pri-

---

66. Gustave Le Bon, *Psychologie des foules*, Paris, 1895, p. 33.
67. Albert Goodwin, *The French Revolution*, pp. 75-77: "The storming and capture of the Bastille on 14th July is one of the best known and least understood events of the revolution. The object of the attackers was not the release of prisoners, but the collection of arms. The actual assault of the fortress was the result of a misunderstanding, and its capture was the achievement, not of the mob, but of the French guards . . . most of the so-called "Conquerors of the Bastille" . . . were small workshop masters and their . . . assistants . . . On 14th July, 1789, the Bastille had a . . . significance for the

marily dominated by irrational factors and not a rational social process determined by the pursuit of self-conscious, commonly understood, ends or purposes. Sartre's rational, teleological account of this historical event is simply not supported by the empirical facts. What was at work in this instance is more like the suggestibility which Le Bon refers to in his account of social dynamics. We do not have to accept Le Bon's notion that individuals, under certain conditions, act like people under hypnosis; but his description of spontaneous group formations in terms of the prominence of unconscious motivating factors, diffusion of suggestibility, and a "contagion of feelings" is both meaningful and plausible.[68]

For Le Bon, the group obeys impulses and feelings which tend to obscure the ostensible rational basis for its formation. A seriality can be transformed into an organized group not only through the intentional acts

---

people of Paris, who were hourly expecting the intervention of the foreign regiments surrounding the city . . . The mob which concentrated round the Bastille . . . did not originally intend to attack it, and, of their two main demands, one at least, the withdrawal of the guns, was granted by the governor . . . before a shot was fired. The fortress was short of supplies and poorly defended, and negotiations for its surrender [were proceeding] between the delegates of the electoral assembly and the governor [who] . . . had promised not to fire upon the crowd while the negotiations were proceeding, unless the fortress was attacked. Two men . . . managed to climb into one of the inner courts and to break the chains of the drawbridge . . . The governor appears to have lost his nerve and the garrison fired. The crowd, thinking that the drawbridge had been lowered by the defenders and suspecting a trap, then began to attack the fortress. A further volley from the garrison, while attempts were being made by delegates from the Hotel de Ville to arrange a parley, strengthened the impression of treachery. Three hundred French guards were dispatched by the municipal authorities and cannon . . . were now employed against the fortress . . . When the fortress eventually fell, its governor was massacred by the crowd in front of the town hall, and . . . the official head of the . . . municipal authority . . . shared the same fate." Cp. Crane Brinton, *The Anatomy of Revolution*, pp. 74-75.

68. Gustave Le Bon, *op. cit.*, pp. 33-35: "In a group every sentiment and act is contagious, and contagious to such a degree that an individual readily sacrifices his personal interest to the collective interest. This is an attitude very contrary to his nature, and of which a man is scarcely capable, except when he makes part of a group . . . an individual immersed for some length of time in a group in action soon finds himself — either in consequence of the magnetic influence given out by the group, or from some other cause of which we are ignorant — in a special state which much resembles the state of 'fascination' in which the hypnotized individual finds himself in the hands of the hypnotizer . . . Under the influence of a suggestion, he will undertake the accomplishment of certain acts with irresistible impetuosity . . . We see, then, that the disappearance of the conscious personality, the predominance of the unconscious personality, the turning by means of suggestion and contagion of feelings and ideas in an identical direction, the tendency to transform immediately the suggested ideas into acts; these, we see, are the principal characteristics of the individual forming part of a group."

of individuals, but by means of the atmosphere of excitement which surrounds and permeates some social movements. The movement from what Simmel called the undifferentiated phase of social relations to a differentiated phase[69] may be the result of an intensification of emotion which is diffused in the seriality and which generates action not through the recognition of a "common idea" or aim, but through the suggestibility and contagion of non-logical factors directing action towards an ambiguous purpose. In addition, the mere success of an activistic minority (e.g., in the case of student rebellions in the United States and France in recent years) can generate a pervasive excitement which stimulates the uncommitted or indifferent to join a group, even though they may not even understand its goals or intentions. What may appear to the outside observer as the intentional action of individuals comprising a group-in-fusion may be the result of an emotional reaction which is then transmitted to other juxtaposed individuals. Vilfredo Pareto's observations in this regard (which are similar to those of Le Bon) are insightful. Pareto maintained that

> Powerful sentiments are for the most part accompanied by certain acts that may have no direct relation to the sentiments but do satisfy a need for action . . . The acts in which sentiments express themselves reinforce such sentiments and may even arouse them in individuals who were without them. It is well known . . . that if an emotion finds expression in a certain physical attitude, an individual putting himself in that attitude may come to feel the corresponding emotion. The residues of this class, accordingly, stand conjoined with emotions, sentiments, and passions in a complex concatenation of actions and reactions.[70]

As an individual becomes a member of a group his conceptions and feelings undergo a subtle transformation: the condition of being-in-a-group may become a significant aspect of the personality of the individual. This would be especially true in religious or political organizations. But the initial nisus towards a group may be dominated by feelings, by a mimetic process, by a contagious reaction.

In regard to the role of the oath *(serment)* in Sartre's account of the evolution of groups, there is a seeming neglect of irrational influences as

---

69. Georg Simmel, *op. cit.*, p. 24: "[In group formations] there . . . exists an initial phase of undifferentiation which, seen from a later, differentiated phase, appears as logically contradictory, but which is thoroughly in line with the undeveloped stage of the organization." Cp. W. McDougall, *The Group Mind*, [Cambridge, 1920] p. 23. McDougall holds that the transformation of a random association of people into an organized (or differentiated) group requires a common interest in an object, a similar emotional 'set' and "some degree of reciprocal influence."
70. Vilfredo Pareto, *The Mind and Society*, trans. A Bongiorno and L. Livingston, New York, 1935, II, p. 647.

well. It is maintained that the individual freely submits to the oath with the intention of solidifying the group. The oath is taken, as it were, in terms of the rational-self-interest of the individual. But Sartre seems to neglect the role that symbols or abstractions (especially enigmatic slogans) play in the unification of groups, a role that takes the place of an oath. Le Bon notes that groups are often unified through the "magical power" of words, of formulae which are chanted or uttered with solemnity by virtue of the generation of powerful collective sentiments which command the loyalty of individuals through a psychological bond.[71] Sartre's general claim that most groups demand an oath of loyalty is quite correct; but he tends to ignore the importance which emotionally charged symbols (or utterances) have in unifying the sentiments of the members of a group. Although he is not unaware of the influence of rituals (or verbalized symbols) on the unification of groups, he tends to minimize the non-rational basis of their cohesive effects. In such cases no commonly shared aim is required, no understanding of an "idea," but only the generally shared attitude towards something or someone, the sentiment of belonging to a group.

Although some of Le Bon's descriptions of group formation and unification may be questionable, some of his observations do point out the importance of irrational (not to say unconscious) factors which can influence the spread of group affiliation. It may be said, however, that Freud's conception of the psychology of groups amplifies the suggestions of Le Bon. In his *Group Psychology and the Analysis of the Ego,* Freud agrees with Le Bon that suggestion or contagion plays a significant role in group formations. But he endeavors to explicate the psychological basis of this suggestibility. Freud avers that individuals yield to the contagion generated by "groups-in-fusion" because this tendency is a form of imitation. Groups, he says, are indeed held together by some "power," but this power is eros. If an individual sacrifices his distinctiveness in a group (for Sartre, becomes a common individual), it is possible that he does this because he feels a need to be in harmony with the group rather than in opposition to it.[72] That is, there are diffuse libidinal ties which characterize groups. To be sure, these

---

71. Gustave Le Bon, *op cit.,* p. 117: "Reason and arguments are incapable of combating certain words and formulas. They are uttered with solemnity in the presence of groups, and as soon as they have been pronounced an expression of respect is visible on every countenance, and all heads are bowed. By many they are considered as natrual forces or as supernatural powers." Le Bon might also have added that reason and arguments are impotent in face of a ritualistic, repetitive use of vitriolic words or phrases.
72. Sigmund Freud, *Group Psychology and the Analysis of the Ego,* p. 31. Cp. pp. 42-43: "In the undisguised antipathies and aversions which people feel toward strangers

libidinal "ties" are sublimated and are not necessarily expressed in any directly erotic ways. As long as a group exists it tends to behave as if it were "uniform," homogeneous. Differences between individuals are tolerated and there is no feeling of aversion towards specific behaviors which may not conform in all details with the ethos of the group. This could be called a deindividuating factor. Freud claims that "such a limitation of narcissism can . . . only be produced by one factor, a libidinal tie with other people."[73] Without relying on Freudian terminology we can say that in groups the tolerance of internal differences does suggest that a "halo effect" is produced by membership in a group which creates a permissive attitude towards members which can not only be derived from a commonly shared aim, idea, or purpose.

Sartre's account of the bond joining together members of a group (with the notable exception of the threat of *terreur*) is too abstract, too intellectualistic. Freud's assertion that the mutual bond which joins together members of a group is an emotionally charged (cathexed) relationship which can be characterized as identification cannot be lightly dismissed. The individual's identification with the group can be a powerful cohesive force. In the military, a strong identification with one's unit is often the basis for good morale. The adoption of a pervasive ethos suggests that something like the process of identification is taking place. Sartre appears to be incorporating such a factor into his account of groups-in-fusion when he refers to the unifying character of a common interest or concern which is directed towards what he calls the "collective entity." However, this collective entity is typically a *material* or *inorganic* entity.[74] His emphasis

---

with whom they have to do we may recognize the expression of self-love — narcissism. This self-love works for the preservation of the individual, and behaves as though the occurrence of any divergence from his own particular lines of development involved a criticism of them and a demand for their alteration . . . when a group is formed the whole of this intolerance vanishes, temporarily or permanently, within the group. So long as a group formation persists or as far as it extends, individuals in the group behave as though they were uniform, tolerate the peculiarities of its other members, equate themselves with them, and have no feeling of aversion toward them." Although Freud mentions the sharing of a common idea as a possible basis for a bond amongst men, he believes that this is not always a strong enough basis for social relationships. As one might expect, he seeks a psychosexual basis — albeit a sublimated basis — for group formations.

73. *Ibid.*, p. 43.
74. W. Desan, *op. cit.*, p. 110. As mentioned previously, Sartre is clearly guided by a predominantly pragmatic model of human action in the *Critique* which places stress upon material privations (needs) and upon a common interest in an instrumental object. The typical social agent Sartre describes is one who has a rational aim, a self-conscious intention or purpose, an awareness of the nature of the negation that is to

upon a material (rather than a psychological) basis for group solidification is basically the result of his assumption that scarcity (a materio-economic factor) is the motivating factor in social processes. Freud's emphasis upon identification is a necessary corrective to Sartre's emphasis upon a rationalistic concern with a material need or a material entity. Freud avers that the intense emotional bonds found in groups account for the reduction of the member of the group to the level of "group individuals" (Sartre's common individual).[75]

If Freud charges that Le Bon neglected the importance of a leader in his explication of the nature of groups, this charge can, with equal force, be made against Sartre. Although he does say that the actions of activists *(l'opération des activistes)* does provide leadership in groups, their activism is said to be an expression of the group's restructuring of itself. The *groupe-en-fusion* has its leader in the "third man regulator" who arises spontaneously from the seriality because of a contingent advantage, psychological or topological.[76] Ostensibly, as groups emerge so, also, do leaders who have an autonomy not granted to other members of the group. In Sartre's terminology the hypothetical "third man" is the mediator of the seriality which was previously "other," each individual alienated from others forming a "multiplicity of epicenters" which was not yet unified. Characteristically, he describes the role of the leaders in abstract terms which seem remote from the concrete emergence of leaders in social processes. For Freud, on the other hand, "the leader is the key figure in group psychology . . . he becomes the individual member's common ego ideal and takes over all the critical faculties."[77] The group "ideal" is embodied

---

be overcome (i.e., negated), etc. This notion of social agents seems to neglect the influence of irrational factors on social action which have been pointed out by numerous sociologists.

75. Sigmund Freud, *op. cit.*, p. 62: " . . . the intense emotional ties which we observe in groups are quite sufficient to explain one of their characteristics — the lack of independence and initiative in their members, the similarity in the reactions of all of them, their reduction, so to speak, to the level of the group individual." Compared to Freud's psychological analysis of the transformation of the individual as he becomes a member of a group Sartre's description is a rationalistic account in the sense that he suggests that an organized group must convert the individual into a common individual in order to avoid diffusion or what Gurvitch calls "destructurization."

76. *CRD*, p. 502. That there are numerous instances when a leader does, in fact, arise spontaneously in a group under certain 'timely' circumstances is undeniable. On the other hand, however, leadership is often conferred upon an individual primarily on the basis of the psychological impact an individual has on a group. In addition, of course, Sartre ought not to exclude the self-conscious pursuit of leadership on the part of energetic or opportunistic individuals.

77. Sigmund Freud, *op. cit.*, xi.

in the leader, the authority figure who dominates others by his charismatic presence, by the power which has been transferred from the group to him. The leader can be the personal objectification of the sovereignty of the group. In regard to him identification is, of course, an important factor. Freud claims that many human beings have a "craving for authority" which requires a personal leader (and not merely the group as a whole).[78] Despite the unfortunate influence which immoral leaders can have, it is clear that the symbolic meaning, the unconscious significance of a leader can have (and has had) an enormous impact upon group unification. Sartre's neglect of this factor in social unification is a serious lacuna in his sociological description.

Although Sartre criticized the Marxists for neglecting the contribution of the projects of individuals to history, he himself tends to conceive of sovereignty primarily in *collective* terms. He seems to by-pass the influence of the prestige of a leader on the process of group formation.[79] The collectivity (with the power of expulsion or punishment) is the ultimate sovereign. Sartre, like Simmel, stresses the negative character of the bond which unifies large groups, the interior norm which becomes more restrictive of individual action as the size of the group increases.[80] The prescription of this interior norm as made coercive through the oath which

---

78. Sigmund Freud, *Collected Papers*, London, 1950, II, p. 290: "Only very few civilized persons are capable of existing without reliance on others or are even capable of coming to an independent opinion. You cannot exaggerate the intensity of man's inner irresolution and craving for authority." It is this assumption which influences the interpretation of group formations which Freud presents in his *Group Psychology and the Analysis of the Ego*.
79. Cp. *The Sociology of Georg Simmel*, ed. K. Wolff, New York, 1964, p. 184: "Prestige lacks the element of super-subjective significance; it lacks the identity of the personality with an objective power or norm. Leadership by means of prestige is determined entirely by the strength of the individual . . . prestige leadership stems from pure personality . . . prestige strikes us as the more voluntary homage to the superior person."
80. Georg Simmel, *op, cit.*, pp. 397-398: "The negative character of the bond that unifies the large group is revealed, above all, in its norms . . . the larger the group is, usually the more prohibitive and restrictive the kinds of conduct which it must demand of its participants in order to maintain itself." Related to this question is the ambiguity, in the *Critique*, concerning the size of the groups Sartre describes. Sartre seems to have only one model in mind in his sociological description; that is, a group of dedicated worker-activists who presumably have as their ultimate finality the transformation of a society which is assumed to be defective in numerous ways. In relation to the question of radical social groups Simmel observes that an increase in the size of such groups (and a corresponding increase in the heterogeneity of such a group) tends to undermine the original radicalism of the core of the group. Georg Simmel, *op. cit.*, pp. 94-95. Sartre seems to be aware of this possibility insofar as he refers to the tendency to stultification and inertia in highly organized social groups, including groups with radical social aims.

sanctions violence seems to yield to the tyranny of the group. Sartre's promulgation of collective sovereignty causes him to transcend the level of descriptive sociology and to propose a *particular* social theory, a revisionist Marxism.[81] His sociology is hardly *wertfrei* in any sense of the term.

Sartre's social phenomenology is defective in a number of respects. First, he passes from an apparent social phenomenology to social prescription thereby violating his own intention in the *Critique*. Second, he neglects the importance of the conferring of consensual power upon a leader[82] (either as activist or as symbolic leader) upon social unification. Third, he seriously neglects the significance of irrational or nonrational factors upon social evolution, upon the individual's commitment to a group. Fourth, he wholly disregards the psychological factors of identification and sublimated cathexis upon group solidarity. Fifth, he undermines his stated intention in his *Critique* to preserve the rights and freedom of individuals and to emphasize the importance of individual *praxis* — his description of

---

81. W. Desan, *op. cit.,* 'p. 250. Cp. W. Odajnyk, *Marxism and Existentialism,* pp. 161-163. While this is obvious to any reader of the *Critique*, there is a sense in which the precise nature of Sartre's commitment to some Marxist principles is difficult to discern. He avers that he is concerned with an analysis of the conditions for the possibility of a social philosophy, with the development of a philosophical anthropology and with an analysis of the concrete, historical individual.

82. Max Weber presented the classic study of the individual who, by virtue of his charismatic qualities, is able to unify diverse groups and provide a sense of direction for many. He described charisma as "a quality of a person which is believed to be unusual ,. . . and on account of which such a person is valued as (equipped) with . . . unusual power and qualities which are not accessible to others." *Wirtschaft und Gesellschaft,* Berlin, 1922, p. 140. Cp. C. J. Friedrich, "Political Leadership and the Problem of the Charismatic Power," *The Journal of Politics,* 23, no. 1, (1961), pp. 3-24. Although the twentieth century has come to know the extreme danger of individuals possessing charismatic qualities — individuals who are themselves irrational or immoral . . . it is clear that such individuals play a significant role in social processes and, hence, cannot be excluded from a complete account of social movements or group unification. The reaction to President Kennedy's assassination in the United States and in Europe is one more indicator of the profound influence that the non-rational, symbolic meaning of a political leader can have on large numbers of people. It was not his actual accomplishments alone — accomplishments which are minimal compared to those of Truman or the unpopular L. B. Johnson . . . which aroused such enthusiasm, but it was, rather, what he "stood for" or symbolized to his admirers. A social phenomenology such as Sartre's should not ignore such relevant phenomena in describing how groups are unified. The irrational or nonrational plays a *positive* as well as a negative role in social organization or unification, in social movements or in what may be called the political teleology of a State. Charisma is a power which can be used for social good as well as for social evil or the creation of a political nihilism. Even the collectivistic, socialistic social organizations Sartre seems to admire were created, to a great extent, by charismatic leaders who were able to

A PHENOMENOLOGY OF SOCIAL RELATIONS 139

the structure and function of groups entirely negates this intention and grants sovereignty to the collectivity or the group alone. Sixth, his entire account of the dialectical process of social relations is fundamentally necessitarian, entirely undermining his ostensible defense of the existentialistic conception of the contingency of human existence and action. Although he criticizes the contemporary Marxists for neglecting the role of the existential projects of the individual, the consequences of his *Critique* are to stress the impotence of the isolated individual and to argue that individual *praxis* is wholly appropriated by the organized practice of the group.

Sartre's description of social relations and processes is valuable insofar as he has shown the complex network of reciprocal interactions among men within a socio-material or practical field and has shown the efficacy of a methodological tool for the interpretation and description of social phenomena: the critical dialectic. Although such an approach to social phenomena is not metaphysically neutral, the conception of experience as dialectical is a view which has heruistic value and which seems more appropriate to social phenomena than purely quantitative or analytic methods of social analysis. This first volume of the *Critique de la raison dialectique* has provided, despite its flaws, the conditions for the possibility of a dialectical sociology, a sociology which reveals the conflicts amongst men and seeks to discover the reason for violence in the human world. Behind the Marxist sentiments which pervade Sartre's social philosophy we can still discern the existential humanist who, despite the sad knowledge he has of the anti-human in man, is still able to hope for a world in which all men will be free and the menace of violence will be permanently negated.

---

transfer their revolutionary zeal to large numbers of people. The "third man regulator" which Sartre discusses is a poor substitute for the dramatic personalities who shape history for good or ill.

SELECTED BIBLIOGRAPHY

This bibliography is a personal selection of Sartre's major philosophical writings and of works which are directly or indirectly related to the subject of this study. It is not intended as a 'complete' bibliography.

Arrow, Kenneth J., "Mathematical Models in the Social Sciences," in *Readings in the Philosophy of the Social Sciences,* ed. May Brodbeck, New York, 1968, pp. 635-667.
Audry, Colette, *Connaissance de Sartre,* Paris, 1955.
Bosserman, P., *Dialectical Sociology,* Boston, 1968.
Brinton, Crane, *The Anatomy of Revolution,* New York, 1965.
Cartwright, D., ed., *Field Theory in Social Science: Selected Theoretical Papers by Kurt Lewin,* New York, 1951.
Cranston, M., *Sartre,* London, 1962.
Desan, W., *The Marxism of Jean-Paul Sartre,* New York, 1965.
Dupré, Louis, *The Philosophical Foundations of Marxism,* New York, 1966.
Durkheim, Emile, *De la Division du Travail,* Paris, 1902.
_____, *Les Régles de la méthode sociologique,* Paris, 1950.
Engels, Frederick, *The Dialectics of Nature,* trans. J. B. S. Haldane, New York, 1940.
Fell, Joseph P., *Emotion in the Thought of Sartre,* New York, 1965.
Freud, Sigmund, *Collected Papers,* London, 1950, II.
_____, *Group Psychology and the Analysis of the Ego,* trans. J. Strachey, New York, 1960.
Friedrich, Carl J., "Political Leadership and the Problem of the Charismatic Power," *The Journal of Politics,* 23, no. 1 (1961).
Friedrichs, R. W., *A Sociology of Sociology,* New York, 1970.
Goodwin, A., *The French Revolution,* New York, 1962.
Gouldner, A., *The Coming Crisis of Western Sociology,* New York, 1970.
Greene, N., *Jean-Paul Sartre: The Existentialist Ethic,* Ann Arbor, 1960.
Gurvitch, Georges, *Déterminismes sociaux et liberté humaine,* Paris, 1955.
_____, *Dialectique et sociologie,* Paris, 1962.
_____, *La vocation actuelle de la sociologie,* Paris, 1950, I.
_____, *L'idée du droit social,* Paris, 1932.
_____, *The Spectrum of Social Time,* trans. M. Korenbaum and P. Bosserman, Dordrecht, Holland, 1964.
Hartmann, Klaus, *Sartre's Ontology,* Evanston, 1966.
_____, *Sartres Sozialphilosophie,* Berlin, 1966.
Hegel, G. W. F., *Phänomenologie des Geistes,* in *Sämmtliche Werke,* ed. G. Lasson, Hamburg, 1907. [*The Phenomenology of Mind,* trans. J. B. Baillie, London, 1931].
Heidegger, Martin, *Sein und Zeit,* Tübingen, 1963.

BIBLIOGRAPHY 141

Husserl, Edmund, *Die Krisis der europäischen Wissenschaften und die transzendentale Phänomenologie*, The Hague, 1954. [*The Crisis of European Science and Transcendental Phenomenology*, Evanston, 1970].
Jeanson, Francis, *Sartre par lui-même*, Paris, 1955.
Jordan, Z. A., *The Evolution of Dialectical Materialism*, New York, 1967.
Kojeve, A., "Hegel, Marx et le Christianisme," *Critique* I, (1946).
Kolakowski, Leszek, "Responsibility and History," in *Existentialism versus Marxism*, ed. G. Novack, New York, 1966.
_____, *Towards a Marxist Humanism*, trans. J.Z. Peel, New York, 1968.
Labedz, L., ed., *Revisionism*, New York, 1962.
Lafarge, Réne, *Jean-Paul Sartre: His Philosophy*, trans. M. Smyth-Kok, Notre Dame, 1970.
Laing, R. D., and D. G. Cooper, *Reason and Violence*, New York, 1964.
Le Bon, Gustave, *Psychologie des foules*, Paris, 1895. [*The Crowd*, New York, 1960].
Lefebvre, Henri, *Le Matérialisme Dialectique*, Paris, 1940.
_____, *L'Existentialisme*, Paris, 1946.
_____, *The Sociology of Marx*, New York, 1968.
Lessing, A., "Marxist Existentialism," *Review of Metaphysics*, XX, (1967).
Lichtheim, G., *Marxism in Modern France*, New York, 1966.
_____, "Sartre, Marxism and History," *History and Theory*, III, no. 2, (1963).
Lukács, G., *Existentialisme ou Marxisme?*, Paris, 1946.
Manser, Anthony, *Sartre: A Philosophic Study*, New York, 1967.
Marcuse, Herbert, "Existentialism: Remarks on J. P. Sartre's *L'Être et le néant*," *Philosophy and Phenomenological Research*, VIII, (1948).
_____, *Reason and Revolution*, Boston, 1960.
Marx, Karl, *Capital*, trans. Eden and Cedar Paul, London, 1933.
_____, *A Contribution to the Critique of Political Economy*, Chicago, 1904.
_____, *Economic and Philosophic Manuscripts of 1844*, trans. M. Milligan, Moscow, 1961.
_____, *The Poverty of Philosophy*, Moscow, n.d.
Marx, K., and F. Engels, *Marx-Engels-Gesamtausgabe*, Moscow, Marx-Engels Institute, eds. D. Rjazanov et al., 1927-1932.
Marx, K., and F. Engels, *The German Ideology*, Parts I and III, New York, 1947.
Marx, K., and F. Engels, *Marx and Engels: Selected Works*, Moscow, 1950.
McBride, W., "Jean-Paul Sartre: Man, Freedom and Praxis," in *Existential Philosophers*, ed. G. A. Schrader, New York, 1967.
McMahon, J. H., *Humans Being: The World of Jean-Paul Sartre*, Chicago and London, 1971.
Merleau-Ponty, M., *Les Aventures de la Dialectique*, Paris, 1955.
Molina, F., *Existentialism as Philosophy*, Englewood Cliffs, 1962.
Möller, J., *Absurdes Sein?*, Stuttgart, 1959.
Murdoch, Iris, *Sartre: Romantic Rationalist*, New Haven, 1953.
Natanson, M., *A Critique of Sartre's Ontology*, Lincoln, Nebraska, 1951.
Novack, G., ed., *Existentialism versus Marxism*, New York, 1966.
Odajnyk, W., *Marxism and Existentialism*, New York, 1965.
Ortega y Gasset, José, *The Revolt of the Masses*, trans. anonymous, New York, 1932.
Pareto, Vilfredo, *The Mind and Society*, trans. A. Bongiorno and A. Livingston, New York, 1935, 3 Vols.
Parsons, Talcott, *Sociological Theory and Modern Society*, New York, 1967.

Plekhanov, George, *The Role of the Individual in History*, trans. anonymous, New York, 1940.
Popper, K. R., *The Open Society and Its Enemies*, London, 1945, II.
Proudhon, P. J., *What Is Property? An Inquiry into the Principles of Right and Government*, trans. B. R. Tucker, London, 1902.
Riesman, David, *Individualism Reconsidered*, New York, 1954.
Ruitenbeek, H. M., *The Individual and the Crowd*, New York, 1964.
_____, *Varieties of Modern Social Theory*, New York, 1963.
Salvan, Jacques, *To Be and Not To Be: An Analysis of Jean-Paul Sartre's Ontology*, Detroit, 1962.
Sartre, Jean-Paul, *Baudelaire*, Paris, 1947.
_____, *Critique de la raison dialectique*, Paris, 1960, I.
_____, *Esquisse d'une théorie des émotions*, Paris, 1939.
_____, *L'Être et le néant*, Paris, 1943, [*Being and Nothingness*, trans. H. Barnes, New York, 1956].
_____, *L'Existentialisme est un humanisme*, Paris, 1946. [*Existentialism*, trans. B. Frechtman, New York, 1947].
_____, *L'Imaginaire*, Paris, 1940.
_____, *L'Imagination*, Paris, 1936.
_____, *Les Mots*, Paris, 1964. [*The Words*, New York, 1964].
_____, *Saint Genet, Actor and Martyr*, New York, 1963.
_____, *Search for a Method*, trans. H. Barnes, New York, 1963.
_____, *Situations*, I-III, Paris, 1947-1949. [*Literary and Philosophical Essays*, trans. A. Michelson, New York, 1955].
_____, *The Transcendence of the Ego*, New York, 1962.
Schaff, Adam, "A Philosophy of Man," in *Existentialism versus Marxism*, New York, 1966.
_____, *Marxism and the Human Individual*, ed. R. S. Cohen, trans. O. Wojtasiewicz, New York, 1970.
Schacht, R., *Alienation*, New York, 1970.
Schuetz, A., "Sartre's Theory of the Alter Ego," *Philosophy and Phenomenological Research*, IX, (1948).
Sheridan, J F., *Sartre: The Radical Conversion*, Athens, Ohio, 1969.
Simmel, Georg, *Conflict* and *The Web of Group Affiliations*, trans. K. Wolff and R. Bendix, Glencoe, 1955.
Sorokin, Pitirim, *Modern Historical and Social Philosophies*, New York, 1963.
_____ and Walter Lunden, *Power and Morality*, Boston, 1959.
Spiegelberg, H., *The Phenomenological Movement*, The Hague, 1960, 2 Vols.
Stack, G. J., "On the Notion of Dialectics," *Philosophy Today*. 15, (1971).
_____, "Sartre's Dialectic of Social Relations," *Philosophy and Phenomenological Research*, XXXI, March (1971).
Stern, A., *Philosophy of History and the Problem of Values*, The Hague, 1962.
_____, *Sartre: His Philosophy and Psychoanalysis*, New York, 1953.
Tiryakian, E. A., *Sociologism and Existentialism*, Englewood Cliffs, 1962.
Tucker, Robert, *Philosophy and Myth in Karl Marx*, Cambridge, 1961.
_____, *The Marxian Revolutionary Idea*, New York, 1969.
Ussher, A., *Journey through Dread*, London, 1955.
Varet, Gilbert, *L'Ontologie de Sartre*, Paris, 1948.
Warnock, Mary, *The Philosophy of Sartre*, London, 1965.

Wolff, K., ed., *The Sociology of Georg Simmel*, New York, 1964.
Zaner, R. M., *The Way of Phenomenology*, New York, 1970.
Zeitlin, I., *Ideology and the Development of Sociological Theory*, Englewood Cliffs, 1968.
——————, *Marxism: A Re-Examination*, London, 1967.

INDEX

"Absolute freedom," 8, 28, 76
Abstract consciousness, 28, 64
Abstract freedom, 8, 16, 23
Activists, 136
Alienation, 46, 71, 94, 113, 114, 124, 126n
"Alter-ego," 40, 41, 62
Analytic reason, 77, 78, 79, 82, 106
Anatomy of Revolution, The, 112n, 132n
"Anthropological Nature," 104
"Antidialectic," 71, 87, 93, 94, 98, 121, 125, 126, 128
Antidialectical negations, 73
"Anti-man," 114
Aristotle, 6, 18
Aron, Raymond, 53
Arrow, K. J., 106n
Astructural phenomena, 58, 63
Aufhebung ("sublation"), 117
"Bad faith," 30
Bastille, the storming of the, 67, 131-132
Being, 10
Being and Nothingness, 3-6, 8, 10, 28, 29, 33, 36, 39-41, 44, 46, 49, 61-65, 70-72, 75, 80, 81, 86, 89, 92, 94, 95, 97-99, 108, 117n, 124n, 129n
Being-for-others, 28, 29-50, 75, 76
"Being-in-itself," 3, 4, 5, 19, 48, 89
Being-in-the-world, 20, 21, 36, 43, 72, 94, 98
Berdyaev, Nicholai, 7
Besoin ("need"), 74, 75, 81, 83, 86, 90, 109n, 111, 112, 116, 130
Black Americans, 112
Body, 20, 22, 31, 32, 33, 34, 37, 64, 75, 86, 98
Bosserman, P., 58n, 68n
"Bourgeois individual," 91
Brinton, C., 112, 132n
Brute existents, 23, 24
Capitalism, 52, 110, 113, 124

Character, 92
Charisma, 138
"Circumspective concern," 71, 109
Class antagonism, 110
"Coefficients of adversity," 21, 23, 24, 43, 49, 62, 70, 72
Collective consciousness, 130
"Collective psyche," 64
Collectivity, 137
Common consciousness, 130
Common danger, 116, 131
Common freedom, 128
"Common individual," 66, 127, 134
Common individual, function of, 124, 127, 130, 136
Common need, 117
Common power, 119, 120, 128
"Communal work," 41
Comprehension ("understanding"), 68-70, 81, 82, 84, 93
Concept of Dread, The, 9
Concept of Nature in Marx, The, 53
Concrete action, 16-28, *passim*
Concrete freedom, 4, 21, 22, 23, 24, 27, 28, 44, 49, 64, 71, 98
Conflict, 114n
Conflict paradigm, 63, 68, 89
Consciousness-body, 20, 21, 71, 75, 86
Consensual power, 138
Constituted dialectic, 80, 87, 118
Constituting dialectic, 80, 87, 93
Contagious reactions, 131, 133, 134
Contingent individual, the, 126n, 127n
Contradictions, 82, 83, 101, 107, 116
Contradictory tensions, 120
Contribution to the Critique of Political Economy, A, 102n
Counterfinality, counterfinalities, 93, 94, 98, 113, 114, 125, 126, 127, 128
"Creator of signs," 70, 102

146 INDEX

Critical dialectic, 77, 101-124, 139
Critique de la raison dialectique (Critique of Rational Dialectic), passim
Crowds, 130ff
Cultural objects, 88, 97
Dasein, 109n
"Das Man" ("one"), 37, 44, 45
De fait groupings, 65 See serialities
Depassement, 82, 116-117
Dependence, 90, 91, 95
"Depth sociology," 58
Desan, W., 11n, 135n, 138n
Determinismes sociaux et liberte humaine, Les, 57, 61n, 62, 69n
Deterministic structure of the world, 61
"Detotalized totality," 20
Diachronic social phenomena, 61, 66, 127
Dialectical analyses, 52
"Dialectical circularity," 60, 112
Dialectical *Existenz,* 107
Dialectical experience, 77, 80, 81, 82, 107, 139
Dialectical materialism, 101-103, 128
Dialectical necessity, 128-129
"Dialectical necessity, 128-129
"Dialectical nominalism," 83
Dialectical reason, 59, 70, 77-85, 124, 125
Dialectical sociology, 56, 57, 61, 62, 76, 84, 99, 139
Dialectical Sociology, 58n, 68n
"Dialectic of life," 51, 126
"Dialectic of nature," 77, 85, 101
Dialectic of *praxis,* 59, 60, 66, 76, 82, 85, 88, 90, 95
Dialectique et Sociologie, 53, 63, 84n, 97n
Dilthey, Wilhelm, 29, 34, 69, 70, 81, 82, 84
Division du Travail, De la, 130n
Dogmatic dialectic, 53n, 77, 85, 100-107
Dominant idea, 120-121
Dupre, L., 129n
Durkheim, E. 63, 64n 92, 105, 130
Dyadic relations, 76
Economic and Philosophic Manuscripts of 1844, 90, 104, 109, 110
Eighteenth Brumaire of Louis Napoleon Bonaparte, The, 52, 125
Engels, F., 77, 85, 102

Erlebnis ("lived experience"), 3, 34, 48, 59, 60, 78, 86, 93
Ethos, 121, 135
"Evanescent contingency," 17
Evolution of Dialectical Materialism, The, 52n
Existentialism versus Marxism, 110, 123n
Existential possibilities, 15
Experiential dialectic, 51
Explanation, 69
Exploitation, 110
"Expressions of life," 29
"Exteriority," 8, 21, 35, 54, 66, 74, 75, 76, 80, 86, 89, 92, 96
Exteriorization of the interior, 80, 86, 129
Facticity, 17, 19, 22, 24, 25, 28, 30, 35, 37, 39, 49, 71, 98, 102, 108, 109, 127, 129
Facticity and freedom, 26
Facticity of consciousness, 17
Faire ("doing"), 21, 50, 108
Finality, 114, 115, 116, 120, 128
Flaubert, G., 91
Fragility, 12, 13
Freedom, 4, 7-10, 15-19, 21-28, 31, 33, 34, 42, 44, 49, 57, 58, 60-62, 64, 66-68, 70-72, 76, 80, 94, 98, 108, 109, 120, 122, 124, 127, 128, 138
Freud, S., 101, 130, 134-137
Genet, J., 33, 37
German Ideology, The, 93, 102, 113
"Global" responsibility, 21
God, 41, 43, 64, 124n
Goodwin, A., 131n, 132n
Greed, 110
Group, coercive power of, 121-124
Group formation, 41, 66, 84, 85, 100-139
Group individual, 136
Group-in-fusion, 116, 117, 133, 134
Group Mind, The, 133n
Group Psychology and the Analysis of the Ego, 134
Gurvitch, Georges, 52-85, 97, 106n, 130
"Halo effect," 135
Hartmann, K., 12, 40, 55n, 61n, 76n, 83n
Hegel, G.W.F., 13, 21, 22, 38, 51, 79, 82, 107, 117, 119, 124, 125, 126, 128, 129
Hegelian, 10, 35, 90, 101-102

INDEX

Hegel's phenomenology, 22, 30, 117, 119n
Heidegger, Martin, 19, 32, 34, 44, 45, 47, 71, 72, 98, 102, 105, 109
Heideggerian, 11, 37
Historical materialism, 77, 87
History and scarcity, 111
History as Absolute, 124
Hobbes, T., 122, 123
Hodological space, 94, 95
"Horizon of possibilities," 18
Human history, 101
"Humanistic Us," 43, 124n
Humans Being, 50
"Human Sciences," 84
Husserl, Edmund, 5, 102
Hyperempiricism, dialectical, 54-57, 86
Hypnosis, 132
Idealization of social agents, 85
Idea of Dialogal Phenomenology, The, 91n
Identification, 135, 136, 138
Imagination, 5, 6
Impersonal social forces, 60
Individuals, 36
Inertial social entities, 60, 66 See "Practico-inert"
Inert matter, 71, 72, 74, 97
Innovative freedom, 57
Intentionality, 5, 7, 9, 10, 61, 80, 86, 93, 102, 104, 107, 108
Interaction of subjectivity and objectivity, 65
Interest, 114
Interiorization of the exterior, 80, 86, 87, 129
Interior norm, 121, 137
Intrasocial freedom, 58
Irrational in social processes, the, 118, 124-139
Irreducible novelty, 78, 79
Jean-Paul Sartre: His Philosophy, 7n
Jordan, Z. A., 52
Kant, Immanuel, 9
Kapital, Das (Capital), 52
Kennedy's assassination, 138n
Kierkegaard, Sren, 8, 9, 25, 51, 126
Kojeve, A., 125n
Kolakowski, L., 52, 123
"Lack," 6, 18, 75, 81, 90, 109, 110, 116

Lafarge, R., 7n
Language, 26-27
Law of totalization, the, 68
Leader, 136-138
Lebenswelt ("life-world"), 101
Le Bon, G., 101, 130-134, 136
Lefebvre, Georges, 55
Lefebvre, Henri, 52, 53, 104, 110n, 117n
Leistungen ("performances"), 5
Les Mots, 33
Lenin, V. I., 123
Le regard ("the look"), 30, 31, 36, 37, 42, 46
Lessing, A., 124
Lewin, K., 94, 118
L'Existentialisme, 117n
Libidinal ties, 134, 135
Lichtheim, G., 107n, 125n
L'idee du droit social, 63n
L'Idiot de la famille, 91
L'Imaginaire, 5
L'Imagination, 5
Literary and Philosophical Essays, 103
Lived-space, 94
"Living totality," 76
"Logic of contradiction," 82
L'Ontologie de Sartre, 61n, 86n
Lukacs, G., 77, 102n, 103n
Macrosociology, 67
Munser, A., 26n
Marcuse, H., 129n
Marx, Karl, 51-54, 71, 73, 90, 93, 94, 101-104, 108-111, 113, 124, 126
Marxism, 3, 51, 53, 54, 84, 87, 89, 100, 101, 103, 114, 123, 138
Marxism and Existentialism, 138n
Marxism and the Existentialists, 53
Marxism and the Human Individual, 53n, 103n, 126n
Marxism in Modern France, 125n
Marxism of Jean-Paul Sartre, The, 111n
Marxist sociology, 101
Marx's dialectic, 52, 53
"Master-slave" relationship, 30, 38
Material dialectic, 100
"Materialism and Revolution," 70, 88, 103
"Materialization" of praxis, 66
Material need, 81, 109, 112, 136

"Material reality," 98
McBride, W., 85
McDougall, W., 133n
McMahon, J., 50n
Meaning, 5, 16, 19, 20, 21, 22, 25, 26, 27, 34, 46, 69, 88, 92, 102, 109
Mechanical order, 78, 106
Mediated reciprocities, 96, 119
Microsociology, 56, 63
Mind and Society, The, 113n
Mitsein ("being-with"), 45, 46, 47, 75
Moreno, J., 118
Narcissism, 134-135
Naturalistic social science, 105
Neant, le, 5
Necessity, necessitarianism, 7, 66, 74, 80, 101, 117, 124-120, 139
"Necessity of Liberty," 127
Need-states, 91
Negative facts, 14
Negativities, 11-15, 72 *passim*
No Exit, 29, 113
Non-reflective consciousness, 10, 48
Non-thetic consciousness, 10, 64, 107n
Nothingness, consciousness as, 4-11
Oath, 119, 122, 128, 133, 134, 137
Objectification, 66, 74, 76, 68, 80, 81, 113
Odajnyk, W., 138n
Ontological conditioning of freedom, 23
Organized group, 66, 120-139
"Original choice," 21
Ossification, 127
"Paradox of freedom," 24
Pareto, V., 130, 133
Parsons, T., 63
Partial determinism, 57, 60, 61, 74, 76, 99
Passive determination, 65
Passivity, 91
Persons, 33, 34, 40, 64
Phenomenological ontology, *passim*
Phenomenology of Mind, The, 21n, 119n
Philosophical anthropology, 84, 122, 138n
Philosophical Foundations of Marxism, The, 129n
Philosophy of Sartre, The, 116n
Plato, 125
Poverty of Philosophy, The, 110
Practical fields, 60, *passim*

"Practical organism," 78
"Practico-inert," 53, 71-74, 96, 97, 105, 125, 126
Praxis, 4, 52n, 53n, 59, 60, 64, 66, 67, 69, 71-75, 78-100, 103-105, 107-109, 111-114, *passim*
"Prenumerical one," 37
Prestige, 137
"Principle of complementarity," 54
Privation, 41, 42
Projects, 16-28, *passim*
Proudhon, P., 107
"Psychic body," 17, 20
Psychological need, 112
Psychologie des foules (The Psychology of Crowds), 131n
Psychophysical individual, 17
"Pure I," the, 63
Questioning, 13, 14
Questions de Methode, 81, 84
Realdialectik, 83
Reason and Revolution, 129n
"Reciprocal imbrication," 35
Reciprocal objectification, 40
"Reef of solipsism, the," 30
Regles de la methode sociologique, Les, 105
Regressive analysis, 11
Regulator, the third man, 136, 139n
Republic, The, 125
Residues, 130, 133
Revolution francaise, La, 55
Revolutions, 111-112
Rumor, 131
Sartre's Ontology, 12n
Sartre's Sozialphilosophie, 55n, 76n
"Scales of determinism," 58
Scarcity, 15, 72, 73, 74, 90, 95, 108-121
Schaff, Adam, 53, 102n, 103n, 110, 126n
Schmidt, Alfred, 53
Schuetz, A., 38n
Sein und Zeit (Being and Time), 32, 44, 102n, 105, 109
Self, 3, 16, 19, 20, 64, 71, 119n
Self-consciousness, 21, 35, 88, 119
Self-realization, 18
Seriality, serialities, 39, 42, 56, 65, 81, 96, 114-116, 125, 132, 136
Simmel, G., 114, 120, 121, 133, 137

INDEX

"Singularized universal," 79
Situation, 17, 19, 20, 22, 24, 28, 39, 40, 42, 44, 60, 61, 64, 65, 69, 71, 84, 85, 87-89, 98, 102, 108
Social classes, 62, 63, 89
Social determinism, 57, 58-76
Social dialectic 51-139, *passim*
Social facts, 92, 93, 105
"Social *Gestalt*," 58
Social phenomena, 85-99, *passim*
Social phenomenology, *passim*
Social psychology, 65
Social relations, phenomenology of, 100-139
Social roles, 47, 64, 65
Social self, 75
Social space, 94
Social time, 61
Sociology, American, 54, 63
Sociology of Georg Simmel, The, 137n
Sociology of Marx, The, 52-53, 104, 111n
Spectrum of Social Time, The, 61n, 64n
Spiritual dialectic, 51
Stack, G., 8n
Strasser, S., 91n
Strawson, P. F., 36
Student rebellions, 133
"Subject-community," 43, 44, 46, 48
Symbols, 134
Terreur ("terror"), 121-124, 128, 135
"Thing-ontology," 98
Things, 92, 96, 105
"Third, the," 38, 39, 41, 42, 43, 45, 75, 76, 95, 96, 117, 136
Totalitarianism, 123
Totality, totalities, 20, 22, 36, 41, 54, 56, 64, 67, 74, 76, 87, 88, 90, 96, 97, 107, 108, 115, 118

"Totality *en marche,*" 59, 67
Totality in process, 20, 22, 59, 108
Totalization, 54, 70, 74, 79, 80, 89, 91, 93-95, 98, 107-109, 112, 113, 120, 124n
Totalization *en cours,* 56, 59, 79, 81, 108
"Total social phenomena," 56, 65, 67, 68, 105
Transcendence of the ego, The, 10
Transcendental justification of dialectical reason, 77, 84
Transformed matter, 80, 89
"Transubstantiation," 89
Truth, 103
Universal history, 129
"Us-object," 39, 41, 42, 43, 46, 48
Varet, G., 61n, 86n
Verstehen ("understanding"), 69, 70, 81, 82
Violence, 122, 128, 139
Vocation actuelle de la sociologie, La, 63n, 67
Vorlesungen uber die Philosophie der Geschichte ("Lectures on the Philosophy of History"), 128
Warnock, M., 116n, 117n, 123n, 126n
Weber, Max, 69, 92, 138n
Web of Group Affiliations, The, 114n
"Web of social roles," the, 64
"We-experience," 91
Wertfrei ("value-free"), 138
"We-subject," 41, 42, 43, 45, 46, 47, 48, 75
"We-world," 32
Worker, 88, 114
World of the Third, the, 39, 41
World, the, 3-29, 31, 32, 34, 35, 42-49, 59, 61, 62, 72, 77, 81, 83, 86, 89, 90, 91, 97, 98, 102, 103, 112, 113
Zuhanden ("utensils"), 34, 43, 60, 102, 109

Gregg Revivals

Contents

Modern Revivals in History
Modern Revivals in Philosophy
Modern Revivals in Economics
Modern Revivals in Military History
Modern Revivals in Sociology
Modern Revivals in African Studies

Forthcoming series

Modern Revivals in Music Studies
Modern Revivals in Economic History

Authors wishing to submit titles for inclusion in any of the listed series should send them to the Editor, Gregg Revivals, White Swan House, Godstone, Surrey RH9 8LW.

Orders to:
Wildwood Distribution Services
Unit 3, Lower Farnham Road, Aldershot, Hants, GU12 4DY

Books are available in hardback only.
All books are in metric Demy 8vo format, 216 × 138 approx, unless otherwise stated.

MODERN REVIVALS IN HISTORY
Series Editor: Michael Collinge

Michael Prestwich
   War, Politics and Finance under Edward I   (0 7512 0000 X)
William Lamont
   Puritanism and the English Revolution
   Vol I: Marginal Prynne, 1600–1669   (0 7512 0001 8)
   Vol II: Godly Rule: Politics and Religion, 1603–1660   (0 7512 0002 6)
   Vol III: Richard Baxter and the Millennium   (0 7512 0003 4)
   Set   (0 7512 0004 2)
Henry Cohn
   The Government of the Rhine Palatinate in the Fifteenth Century   (0 7512 0005 0)
Robin Law
   The Oyo Empire c. 1600–c. 1836: A West African imperialism in the era of the Atlantic Slave Trade   (0 7512 0006 9)
Jeremy Black
   The English Press in the Eighteenth Century   (0 7512 0007 7)
Patrick Joyce
   Work, Society and Politics: the culture of the factory in later Victorian England   (0 7512 0008 5)
Keith Middlemas
   Diplomacy of Illusion: The British Government and Germany, 1937–1939   (0 7512 0009 3)
Charles Brand
   Byzantium confronts the West, 1180–1204   (0 7512 0053 0)
John Kenyon
   Robert Spencer Earl of Sunderland 1641–1702   (0 7512 0055 7)
Peter Thomas
   The House of Commons in the Eighteenth Century   (0752 0054 9)

Doreen Rosman
  Evangelicals and Culture   (0 7512 0056 5)
Avner Offer
  Property and Politics 1870–1914: Landownership, Law, Ideology and Urban Development in England   (0 7512 0066 2)
Robert McKenzie
  British Political Parties: The Distribution of Power within the Conservative and Labour Parties   (0 7512 0067 0)

Forthcoming

Peter Dickson
  The Financial Revolution in England: a study of the development of public credit, 1688–1756   (0 7512 0010 7)

MODERN REVIVALS IN PHILOSOPHY
Series Editor: Dr David Lamb

David Archard
  Marxism and Existentialism: The Political Philosophy of Sartre and Merleau-Ponty   (0 7512 0051 4)
L Jonathan Cohen
  The Probable and the Provable   (0 7512 0011 5)
David E Cooper
  Authenticity and Learning: Nietzche's Educational Philosophy   (0 7512 0012 3)
Jorge A Larrain
  Marxism and Ideology   (0 7512 0013 1)
Jorge A Larrain
  A Reconstruction of Historical Materialism   (0 7512 0048 4)
Jorge A Larrain
  The Concept of Ideology   (0 7512 0049 2)
D G C Macnabb
  David Hume: His Theory of Knowledge and Morality   (0 7512 0014 X)
Richard J Norman
  Hegel's Phenomenology: A Philosophical Introduction   (0 7512 0015 8)
Anthony O'Hear
  Experience Explanation and Faith (new introduction)   (0 7512 0052 2)
John O'Neill
  Sociology as a Skin Trade: essays towards a reflexive sociology   (0 7512 0016 6)
John O'Neill (ed)
  Modes of Individualism and Collectivism   (0 7512 0050 6)
Stephen Priest (ed)
  Hegel's Critique of Kant   (0 7512 0064 6)
R A Sharpe
  Contemporary Aesthetics   (0 7512 0017 4)
George J Stack
  Kierkegaard's Existential Ethics   (0 7512 0018 2)
George J Stack
  Sartre's Philosophy of Social Existence   (0 7512 0058 1)
W H Walsh
  Metaphysics   (0 7512 0019 0)
W H Walsh
  Reason and Experience   (0 7512 0020 4)
Deirdre Wilson
  Presuppositions and Non-Truth–Conditional Semantics   (0 7512 0021 2)

MODERN REVIVALS IN ECONOMICS
Series Editor: Professor Mark Blaug

Mark Blaug
　An Introduction to the Economics of Education　(0 7512 0022 0)
Mark Casson
　The Entrepreneur: An Economic Theory　(0 7512 0023 9)
Mark Casson
　Multinationals and World Trade: Vertical Integration and the Division of Labour in World Industries　(0 7512 0024 7)
A J Culyer
　The Political Economy of Social Policy　(0 7512 0025 5)
John Cullis and Peter West
　The Economics of Health: An Introduction　(0 7512 0026 3)
G C Harcourt
　Some Cambridge controversies in the theory of capital　(0 7512 0027 1)
Ian Steedman
　Fundamental Issues in Trade Theory　(0 7512 0028 X)
Carl Shoup
　Ricardo on Taxation　(0 7512 0060 3)
Melvin L Greenhut
　A Theory of the Firm in Economic Space　(0 7512 0074 3)

MODERN REVIVALS IN MILITARY HISTORY
Series Editor: Professor Brian Bond

Brian Bond
　Liddell Hart: a study of his Military Thought (new preface)　(0 7512 0029 8)
Michael Howard
　Studies in War and Peace　(0 7512 0030 1)
Charles Carrington
　Soldier from the Wars Returning (new preface)　(0 7512 0031 X)
Sir Ian Hamilton
　The Soul and Body of an Army (new preface)　(0 7512 0032 8)
Sir William Robertson
　Soldiers and Statesmen, (new preface) (2 vols)
　Vol I　(0 7512 0033 6)
　Vol II　(0 7512 0034 4)
　Set　(0 7512 0035 2)
Charles à Court Repington
　The First World War, (new preface) (2 vols)
　Vol I　(0 7512 0036 0)
　Vol II　(0 7512 0037 9)
　Set　(0 7512 0038 7)
Spenser Wilkinson
　The Rise of General Bonaparte (new preface)　(0 7512 0039 5)
Spenser Wilkinson
　Moltke's Military Correspondence, 1870-1871 (new preface)　(0 7512 0040 9)
Spenser Wilkinson
　The French Army Before Napoleon (new preface)　(0 7512 0043 3)
I S Bloch
　Is War Now Impossible? Being an Abridgement of the War of the Future in its Technical, Economic and Political Relations　(0 7512 0041 7)
R J Minney
　The Private Papers of Hore-Belisha　(0 7512 0042 5)

Sir Archibald Wavell
Allenby: A Study in Greatness (new preface)   (0 7512 0061 1)
Allenby in Egypt (new preface)   (0 7512 0062 X)
Set: (0 7512 0063 8)

MODERN REVIVALS IN SOCIOLOGY
Series Editor: Professor Chris Bryant

Chris Jenks (ed)
The Sociology of Childhood: Essential Readings   (0 7512 0044 1)
Zygmunt Bauman
Hermeneutics and Social Science: Approaches to Understanding   (0 7512 0045 X)
Howard Parker
View From The Boys: A Sociology of Down-Town Adolescents (new preface)
(0 7512 0046 8)
Nicholas Spykman
The Social Theory of Georg Simmel   (0 7512 0047 6)
Daniel Lawrence
Black Migrants: White Natives. A Study of Race Relations in Nottingham
(0 7512 0057 3)
Peter Halfpenny
Positivism and Sociology: Explaining Social Life   (0 7512 0059 X)
William Outhwaite & Michael Mulkay (eds)
Social Theory and Social Criticism: Essays for Tom Bottomore   (0 7512 0073 5)

Forthcoming

Gaston Rimlinger
Welfare Policy and Industrialization in Europe, America and Russia   (0 7512 0068 9)

MODERN REVIVALS IN AFRICAN STUDIES
Series Editor: Anthony Kirk-Greene

Geoffrey Kay (ed)
The Political Economy of Colonialism in Ghana: A Collection of Documents and
Statistics, 1900-1960 (new introduction)
(0 7512 0079 4)
E A Brett
Colonialism and Underdevelopment in East Africa: The Politics of Economic Change,
1919-1939   (0 7512 0080 8)
Colin Newbury
British Policy Towards West Africa: Select Documents
Vol I: 1786-1874
Vol II: 1875-1914 (with Statistical Appendices 1800-1914)
Set (0 7512 0084 0)
Christopher Fyfe
A History of Sierra Leone (new introduction)   (0 7512 0086 7)
Christopher Fyfe
Africanus Horton: West African Scientist and Patriot (new introduction)
(0 7512 0085 9)
Martin S Kisch
Letters and Sketches from Northern Nigeria (new introduction)   (0 7512 0087 5)